THE JUICE LOVER'S
BIG BOOK
of JUICES

425 RECIPES FOR SUPER NUTRITIOUS AND CRAZY DELICIOUS JUICES

THE JUICE LOVER'S
BIG BOOK
of JUICES

Vanessa Simkins

HARVARD COMMON PRESS

Brimming with creative inspiration, how-to projects, and useful information to enrich your everyday life, Quarto Knows is a favorite destination for those pursuing their interests and passions. Visit our site and dig deeper with our books into your area of interest: Quarto Creates, Quarto Cooks, Quarto Homes, Quarto Lives, Quarto Drives, Quarto Explores, Quarto Gifts, or Quarto Kids.

First published in the United States of America in 2016 by
The Harvard Common Press, an imprint of The Quarto Group,
100 Cummings Center, Suite 265-D, Beverly, MA 01915, USA.
T (978) 282-9590 F (978) 283-2742
QuartoKnows.com

The Harvard Common Press titles are also available at discount for retail, wholesale, promotional, and bulk purchase. For details, contact the Special Sales Manager by email at specialsales@quarto.com or by mail at The Quarto Group, Attn: Special Sales Manager, 401 Second Avenue North, Suite 310, Minneapolis, MN 55401, USA.

20 19 18 17 16   4 5

ISBN: 978-1-55832-855-6
Electronic edition published in 2017.

Library of Congress Cataloging-in-Publication Data available.

Design: Elizabeth Van Itallie
Cover Image: Vanessa Simkins
Photography: Vanessa Simkins, except for the photos on pages 8 and 352, which were taken by Jennifer Knapp

Printed in China

The effects of the ingredients and recipes in this book on health and wellness will vary from person to person. There are many variables that play a role in your health. Always consult a physician about your health, wellness, medical conditions, and dietary needs. Always consult with your doctor on any health questions, reactions, or concerns you may have regarding the effects of ingredients and recipes. Recipes are not meant to cure, treat, or diagnose health issues or diseases. The health-related information provided in this work is based on the author's research on nutrition and on her personal experience.

MIX
Paper from responsible sources
FSC® C008047
www.fsc.org

To my *All About Juicing* fans: This book is dedicated to you.
Without your support and loyalty, this book wouldn't be possible.

And to Adam, Mom, Dad, Derek, and Anne:
Thanks for your encouragement, support, love, and laughter, and for taste testing
my juicing experiments throughout this amazing journey.

CONTENTS

Preface 8

JUICING BASICS   11

VEGETABLES

Vegetable Juices 29
Green Juices 50
Herbal Juices 72

FRUITS

Fruit Juices 95
Citrus Juices 118
Tropical Juices 140
Lemonades 157

SPECIALTY JUICES

Chia Juices 177
Nut Milk Juices 193
Kid-Friendly Juices 212

ESPECIALLY FOR HEALTH

Energy Juices 229
Calming Juices 240
Cleansing Juices 248
Slimming Juices 257
Juice Shots 268

AND MORE

Party Punches 293
Juice Sodas 289
Blender Juices 315

Acknowledgments 340
About the Author 341
Index 342

PREFACE

No one loves juice more than I do. I've been juicing for close to fifteen years now and I continue to find it a wonderful part of my daily lifestyle. I still remember how excited I was when I received my first juicer on my doorstep and what it was like to make and drink my first apple and carrot juice. It was love at first taste, and I've never stopped.

If you know me, you know that my

purpose is to encourage people to juice for health every day. I share this message with my own online communities on all-about-juicing.com and vanessasjuiceclub.com, and now, with this book, I look forward to reaching a wider audience. Juicing is a great supplement to a healthy diet and makes a real difference in people's lives. It's why I love juicing and why I continue to strive to inspire others to juice.

I still get excited when I make new recipes for my readers. And it brings tears to my eyes when I hear from readers who say that juicing has changed their lives, as it did mine. I am both thrilled and honored to know that my readers take the advice I had to learn the hard way (so you don't have to) and use the recipes I've tested in my kitchen.

My ultimate wish is that this book will give you the assistance you need to make juicing a way of life. From my point of view, juicing is not a fad, a trend, or something to do for a short period of time. Juicing is a lifestyle, and I want to help you make it so.

This juicing book will take you through secrets that have taken me years to uncover. It will help you feel comfortable with juicing as you make it a part of your daily lifestyle. And if you're already an avid juicer, it will push you beyond your limits.

Here's what you will learn:

- How to choose a juicer as well as other handy kitchen tools

- The difference between blending and juicing, so you know which is better for your own goals

- How to create tasty vegetable, fruit, citrus, and green juice combinations that will make you smile instead of grimace

- My list of the top produce for juicing

- Tips on boosting your juice with natural potent additives

- How to make juice shots for enhancing immunity, energy, and glowing skin

- How to juice for energy and stamina

- How to make party punches for your guests

- The details on making the best juice sodas and spritzers

- Why chia juices are all the rage now and how to make your own

- How to make creamy nut milk juices

- The details on how to make tropical juices for the days you need to escape to an island

- How to properly use herbs in your juices

- What to juice to calm your nerves or to prepare for a good night's sleep

- How to use your blender to make blended juice when a juicer isn't available

- How to make juices that your kids really will want to drink

- How to prepare slimming juices to help you fit into your skinny jeans

How to Use This Book

Throughout this book, I'll provide tasty recipes and lots of extra "Juicy Tips" to help you navigate your juicing adventures. Recipes can be tweaked to your own liking. Some you'll like, and some you'll probably want to change. That's okay. Be free and wild: Take my creations and change them up to make them your own. It's okay to use kale instead of spinach or an apple instead of a pear. Juicing isn't an exact science like baking, and it never will be. The juice police will not come after you.

If you are new to juicing, my advice would be to try a few of the recipes first exactly as they are written. Then, once you get the hang of how juices taste and what your palate likes, modify the recipes from there. Green juices can be the most finicky. Lean toward using fewer greens if you are a newbie and experiment with different greens. Don't give up if you don't like juicing at first. It takes time to discover your own palate. Remember that if the final drink tastes good to you, then it's a success.

Here are some other points you should know as you work your way through the book:

It doesn't matter what kind of juicer you have, as long as you have one. Don't worry about getting a high-end juicer until you are sure you are going to love juicing.

Sometimes vegetable juices need a small addition of some fruit to make them palatable. This is why you'll find some fruits included in the vegetable recipes.

Juicing is not a one-stop cure-all for all health problems. There are many factors that contribute toward a healthy body. A healthy lifestyle includes proper hydration, good sleep, stress management, and proper nutrition. Juicing can make a tremendous difference in bridging the nutritional gaps in one's diet, and this often leads to improved health and weight loss for many people.

One of the most common questions I get about juicing has to do with the sugar content of juices. Remember that the sugar in juices is natural sugar, which is not the same as refined sugar. Fresh, raw juice has natural sugar along with other nutrients and enzymes. If you're worried about sugar, talk to your doctor and stick to vegetable-based juices or dilute your fruit juices with water or coconut water. As a general rule, it's a good idea to drink your vegetables and eat your fruits. But juicing fruits is always healthier than eating that slice of chocolate cake.

Serving sizes vary. This happens because different people like to drink different amounts of juice and also because produce ingredients rarely come in uniform sizes. My cucumber might be larger and juicier than yours, so it will yield a different amount of juice. When size is important to the balance of flavors in a juice, I will specify the size in the ingredients. Keep this in mind as you make the juices and feel free to add more or less of any of the ingredients to make a juice to your liking.

I love you, Juice Lovers, and thank you for allowing me into your juice kitchen. Enjoy these juices.

Love + Juice,
Vanessa

JUICING BASICS

Why We Juice

The principle of juicing might seem complicated, but it's really quite simple. Consuming nutrient-rich juice from fruits and vegetables is the best way to give our bodies quality nutrition in a way they can absorb quickly and easily.

Our bodies need good fuel to operate at an optimal level. Good fuel for our bodies is pure food that includes an abundance of fruits, vegetables, and greens. The vital nutrients in produce are not something we can skimp on. If we are deficient in just one nutrient, it can throw our delicate systems out of whack, causing inflammation and eventually disease. Our bodies are constantly cleansing, constantly creating new cells, and constantly fighting against toxins, and each of these tasks depends

on the fuel we consume to carry out these daily functions. When your body has the nutrients it needs, it operates at its highest level. Here are some other important reasons why we juice:

Commercially produced juices often have added sugars, flavors, and preservatives. They are also heated as they are produced, which destroys delicate nutrients and precious enzymes. By juicing fresh produce in your own kitchen, you avoid these potentially harmful additives and you don't lose nutrients through heating. On top of that, you can tailor the juices to your own tastes and health needs.

By juicing fresh produce in your own kitchen, you avoid potentially harmful additives and you don't lose nutrients through heating.

Juicing helps your body absorb and metabolize the nutrients in fresh produce. Freshly prepared fruit or vegetable juice contains the same types and amounts of nutrients as the whole produce it's prepared from, but those nutrients are easier to absorb and metabolize when they're already in liquid form. Think of it like an IV into your bloodstream. Your body doesn't have to digest the fiber that's in the solid vegetable; it only has to absorb the liquid nutrients.

Juicing can help you get the recommended daily servings of fruits and vegetables. It also helps us achieve a more varied, interesting, and nutritionally balanced diet. Most people tend to eat only a few different types of fruits and vegetables, but juicing allows us to consume greater amounts of different produce.

Because juicing assists us in getting an abundance of raw, fresh produce into our diet, it can boost the immune system, aid digestion, alleviate allergies, help reduce blood pressure, improve circulation, slow aging, and enhance energy levels.

New nutrients are discovered regularly. Fresh produce contains nutrients that haven't been discovered and that can help our bodies in ways we aren't even aware of yet. While vitamin supplements are widely available today, the only nutrients you will get in a vitamin supplement are the ones that have been discovered and named.

Juicing allows you to enhance your diet with naturally occurring nutrients, not nutrients manufactured in a lab.

The Difference Between Juicing and Blending

The similarities and differences between juicing and blending can cause a lot of confusion. Many people think they are the same, or they are unclear about what true "juice" is. Both juicing and blending can be extremely beneficial for our diets, but they are vastly different.

Juicing is the process of extracting the nutrient-rich liquid from the fiber of fresh fruits and vegetables. You need a juicer machine to make true juice.

Blending is the process of mixing fresh produce, which includes the juice and the fiber, into a drink, often called a smoothie or a blender juice. You need a blender to make these drinks.

When we drink juice and your body doesn't have to digest the fiber, it quickly absorbs the nutrients so that you can use that nutrition right away to heal and detoxify. Juicing breaks down the cells of the produce and unlocks the nutrients for easier absorption, something that our teeth and digestive systems do when fiber is present. The fiber in fruits and vegetables, in other words, can slow down the digestive process.

Juicing allows us to get a greater amount of nutrition in a smaller glass because this fiber is extracted. For example, if you juiced a small bag of carrots, you would be left with a large glass of delightfully sweet juice that your body can absorb rapidly. If you were to blend a small bag of carrots, you would have much more to drink and it would be thick and unappetizing. It would also take a little bit longer for your body to absorb and assimilate that blended drink.

This is why juicing has been used for years by top practitioners to support the healing of many ailments and serious diseases. I might add that juicing strong-tasting vegetables, like bell peppers or asparagus, yields a milder and tastier drink than you would get if you blended them. On the other hand, blending is great for produce that can't be juiced, such as bananas or avocados, or for high-sugar produce, which can benefit from retaining the fiber to prevent blood sugar spikes.

You can't make true juice in a blender, but you can make juice-like beverages that I call "blender juices." See the chapter that begins on page 315 for examples. Blender juices are great for people who do not own a juicer. They are juice-like beverages, too, for people who have a blender but want something lighter than a smoothie.

I don't believe one method is necessarily better than the other. I juice and blend juices daily and encourage you to do the same. As you might imagine, I prefer juicing to blending on most days. I feel it is the easiest, fastest way for my body to assimilate nutrients and gain the most benefits from the fresh fruits and vegetables in my diet.

Juicers

There are several types of juicers and many brands of juicers on the market. There is a lot of debate on which juicers are best. The decision about which juicer to buy can be confusing because there are so many choices available.

The first thing you'll want to decide is the type of juicer that fits your wants and needs. Your juicer options are a *centrifugal juicer*, a *single-gear juicer*, a *twin-gear juicer*, a *hydraulic press juicer*, and a *manual juicer*.

Here is an overview of each type to help make your decision easier. It's important to remember that having and using any juicer is better than not having one at all.

CENTRIFUGAL JUICERS

Centrifugal juicers use a spinning technique to extract juice from the fiber. The machine cuts the produce and then spins it up against a mesh screen that captures the pulp and allows the juice to pass through the screen.

Centrifugal juicers are the most common and inexpensive ones on the market. They are less versatile than gear juicers and tend to have a shorter life span. One major downside to these juicers is that the fast spinning creates high friction, and therefore heat, which can damage delicate enzymes and nutrients and cause the juice to spoil faster. Juice from these machines will not keep for longer than 8 hours. These juicers produce a watery pulp and have a lower juice yield compared to other machines.

Still, a centrifugal juicer is a great option if you are new to juicing, especially if you aren't sure if you are going to like juicing or if you aren't into the idea of spending a lot of money on kitchen appliances.

SINGLE-GEAR JUICERS

Single-gear juicers are also called masticating juicers. They are a step above centrifugal juicers and a step below twin-gear juicers. They have an auger that cuts and crushes the produce as they make juice. This process is slower than a centrifugal juicer, but on the positive side, it is less likely to destroy delicate nutrients and enzymes. There is a higher juice yield and slower spoilage as compared to centrifugal models. Juice from these machines can keep for up to 24 hours. These juicers are versatile. Many common models make baby food, nut butters, ice creams, and tomato sauce. Some of them can juice wheatgrass.

Single-gear juicers typically have excellent longevity and are the best value for the money. They have strong motors and a durable design. The most important thing to remember about these machines is that the slow juicing technique they use for juicing preserves the nutrients to serve up optimum nutrition as compared to a centrifugal machine.

TWIN-GEAR JUICERS

Most veteran juicers agree that triturating twin-gear juicers are the best household models. These juicers have two gears that crush the produce at a low speed for the best output possible. Because the juicer is crushing the produce slowly, and not spinning, it creates very little friction, and therefore almost no heat, so that it does not damage delicate nutrients and enzymes. Juice made from these juicers can keep for up to 36 hours, which can be convenient. Twin-gear juicers also create a higher juice yield with dry pulp, ensuring you get the most juice out of your produce.

Twin-gear juicers tend to be on the more expensive side, but they are worth the money if you want the best nutrition, value, and versatility in a juicer. They juice both hard and soft produce well, including wheatgrass. Twin-gear juicers also have the ability to homogenize to make nut butters, baby food, ice cream, and pastas.

HYDRAULIC PRESS JUICERS

These juicers use a triturating technique followed by a hydraulic press method. These juicers juice slowly and produce the highest quality available. They are often too pricey for the average household juicer, as they cost thousands of dollars. For that reason, although they are a superior type of juicer, they are used mostly for commercial use and are what you'll see in juice bars. Juicers that fall in this category include the famous Norwalk brand.

MANUAL AND WHEATGRASS JUICERS

Manual juicers are, as their name suggests, hand operated and can only be used for citrus juices or wheatgrass. Their functionality is limited, but they are good for small juicing

jobs. A manual juicer can be referred to as a citrus juicer, but it can also be a hand-crank model that is mainly used for wheatgrass. Some people use hand-crank wheatgrass juicers for juicing fruits and vegetables while traveling because the juicers are compact and can be easily packed into a suitcase. Though this is effective, it's also time-consuming, and I find it easier to hit up a local juice bar if I want juice while out of town.

If you are looking to juice only wheatgrass, it's nice to have a stand-alone model, especially if you juice wheatgrass in abundance. In addition to the hand-crank models, there also are electric juicers made specifically for wheatgrass.

Other Tools for Your Juice Kitchen

For juicing, all you really need is a juicer and some basic knives. However, there are a few other handy items you might want to help make it a fun and easy experience.

• Cutting boards. I love very large wood, bamboo, or plastic cutting boards, and they are essential if you will be juicing often or in large quantities. I need a lot of space when I am juicing, so sometimes I'll use two at once.

• Glass straws. I love my pretty glass straws. They are a fun way to drink juice without the plastic waste.

• Mason jars and other glass containers. If you are unable to drink your juices right away, you'll need something to store them in. Glass is preferable to plastic or other materials. Luckily, there is an abundance of airtight glass jars in many shapes and sizes available today. Mason jars are cheap, easy to open and close, and great for traveling. They are what I use most often to drink and store my juice.

• Measuring bowl or cup. A measuring bowl or cup is handy if you want to know how much juice a given recipe makes or if would like to control your portions.

• Peeler. A peeler isn't necessary for most juices, but it is a great tool for removing citrus rinds. If your produce isn't organic, you can use a peeler to remove the skin and reduce the quantity of pesticides you consume.

• Salad spinner. It's never any fun to wash leafy greens for your green juices. Salad spinners make cleaning lettuce and leafy greens extremely easy.

• Sharp knives. Quality knives are a good investment because most of the produce you will be juicing needs to be cut first. I use a paring knife, an 8-inch (20 cm) chef's knife, and my serrated bread knife often.

• Strainer. Strainers can be helpful if your juice is thick and you'd like to remove some of the fine pulp that might have seeped in during the juicing process. I prefer to drink my juice as is, but many people strain their beverage after it's juiced, simply because they prefer a watery juice. Stainless steel strainers are the most popular, but nut milk bags work just as well.

• Vegetable brush. Vegetable brushes are great tools for scrubbing fruits and vegetables clean prior to juicing them. They are also great for cleaning out your juicer's mesh screen and other small pieces of the machine when you're done juicing.

• Vinegar soak. If you want to make a simple homemade fruit and vegetable soak, you'll need white vinegar and water. Fill your sink or a large bowl with warm water and add ¼ cup (60 ml) of white vinegar. Let your fruits and veggies sit for 15 minutes and then rinse.

Juice Boosters

There are some fabulous extras you can use to supercharge your juices to make them more potent. I call them "juice boosters." Using them is my secret way to make a juice more pleasant and fun to drink. Depending on which ones you use, they also up the ante on the antioxidant, chlorophyll, fiber, weight loss, and beautifying properties of your already healthy drink. While I don't add juice boosters to my juice every day, they are great

to incorporate into your juicing routine every now and then.

• Aloe. Aloe is not just for topical use. It is extremely healing when consumed internally. I find it's easy to scrape a fresh aloe leaf and mix it into a juice with a spoon or to add 1 to 2 tablespoons (15 to 28 ml) of a good-quality store-bought inner-leaf aloe juice to your drink.

• Avocado. Avocados themselves cannot be juiced in a juicer. But avocado can taste de-lightful when blended into a juice. Avocados add healthy fats to your diet and are high in vitamin E. Add ¼ of an avocado to your juice drink and blend in a blender to combine.

• Cayenne pepper and bottled hot sauces. Both are a great addition to many vegetable juices and juice shots, including those that in-clude tomatoes. Chile peppers contain capsaicin, which is highly anti-inflammatory and pain relieving and helps support healthy metabolism. Try adding a few drops of hot sauce or a few shakes of cayenne to your next vegetable juice.

Chile peppers contain capsaicin, which is highly anti-inflammatory and pain relieving and helps support healthy metabolism.

• Chia seeds. Chia seeds have an amazing amount of nutrients and very few calories. They were a major food staple for the Mayans and Aztecs. They are high in fiber, protein, omega-3 fatty acids, and antioxidants. Add 1 tablespoon (13 g) to your glass of juice. Although they are flavorless, they will absorb water in the juice and turn it into a thick gel-like drink that will keep you full.

• Coconut milk. Make any drink creamy and tropical with the addition of coconut milk. I like to add 1 to 2 tablespoons (15 to 28 ml) and mix it with a spoon. Coconut milk boasts nutrients such as lauric acid, which has antibacterial, antifungal, and antiviral properties. It also has healthy fats essential for heart health and for healthy skin and hair.

• Coconut water. Coconut water can turn a simple fruit juice or green juice into a flavorful and hydrating tropical drink. Coconut water's electrolyte properties and nutrients are superb. Add ½ cup (120 ml) to your fruit, veggie, or green juices to reap its benefits and enhance the taste. If you prefer low-sugar juices, use coconut water in place of fruit in your green or vegetable recipes.

• Flax seeds. Flax seeds add extra fiber and nutrients to your diet. They also are popular for those trying to control cholesterol levels. Add ½ teaspoon of finely ground flax seeds to each serving of juice and mix it with a spoon.

• Garlic. Garlic is highly antibacterial and anti-inflammatory. Its flavor in juice is strong, but if you need some antibiotic power, throw a fresh garlic clove into your vegetable juice recipe.

• Ginger. Ginger supports healthy digestion and immunity. It also enhances the flavor of your juices. Use a ½- to 1-inch (1.2 to 2.5 cm) piece of ginger in your juices.

• Herbs. Fresh herbs have been used medicinally and to enhance cuisine for many centuries. They have special nutrients that are beneficial to our health. For example, rosemary may help relieve headaches, and cilantro may help to remove heavy metals from the body. While they typically have strong flavors, they can be juiced in small amounts.

• Lemons and limes. Lemons and limes can disguise strong flavors in a juice, in addition to being powerhouses of nutrition. Throw in ½ to 1 lemon or lime without the peel to enhance flavor and gain the fruit's benefits. If you want an immunity boost, leave the peel on because its essential oils can help boost your internal defense system.

• Maca powder. Maca is a plant from Peru that is used for enhancing energy, memory, performance, and fertility. Add this superfood supplement to your juice buy mixing in ¼ to ½ teaspoon of the powder.

• Nut milks. The addition of a nut milk to your juice transforms it into a creamy, sweet, and filling beverage. It's a palatable way to gain the benefits from nuts.

• On the rocks. Juice served on ice is surprisingly refreshing. It's also a great way to help you reach your ideal daily water intake and to add extra refreshment.

• Psyllium husk. Psyllium is a natural dietary fiber supplement available in powdered form. Many people also use it to help lower cholesterol levels. It has no flavor but does thicken in water. If you want extra fiber and cholesterol-lowering benefits, mix 1 teaspoon into a serving of juice.

• Salt and pepper. Salt and pepper can add another level of flavor to your juices. Add a shake of pink Himalayan salt to your tomato juice or shake ground pepper over a carrot juice. You might like it.

• Sparkling water. Sparkling water can instantly add a little personality to your juice and make more like a soda. Adding sparkling water is a great way to dilute sugary juices and enhance your juice drink. Add ½ cup (120 ml) to a serving of juice.

• Spirulina. Spirulina is a sea vegetable high in natural chlorophyll and iodine. It is sold in health food stores in dried powder form. It mixes great in smoothies or juices and is a wonderful supplement to support detoxification. Add 1 teaspoon to each serving of juice.

• Stevia. Stevia is a natural sweetener made from a plant of the same name. You can purchase it in liquid drops or dried powder form. It can be used to naturally sweeten your juice in a way that will not cause your blood sugar to spike. Add a few drops or a shake of powder to your juice drink to sweeten it.

• Turmeric. Turmeric is an amazing addition to almost any juice. It doesn't have a strong flavor when juiced, but it is packed with anti-inflammatory and immune-building nutrients. Add 1 to 3 inches (2.5 to 7.5 cm) of the fresh root to your juices.

Turmeric doesn't have a strong flavor when juiced, but it is packed with anti-inflammatory and immune-building nutrients.

• Wheatgrass powder. Wheatgrass is an amazing grass with numerous health benefits. While you can juice it, you can also buy it in powder form. Add 1 tablespoon (8 g) to your serving of juice and stir to combine.

Insider Juicing Tips

It took me years of experimenting to uncover these best practices for juicing, and I'm so glad to pass them on to you. Follow this advice to make juicing a pleasant and fun experience.

• Don't be afraid to experiment with produce combinations. Juicing is like cooking. Sometimes your creations turn out tasty and sometimes they don't—and that's okay. It takes time to develop a palate for some juices.

• When making your own recipes, use a 3:1 ratio. If you're confused about making your own tasty recipes, use a recipe formula of three vegetables to one fruit. In most cases, this will ensure a well-balanced juice that is neither too sweet nor too "green" tasting.

• Consume juice on an empty stomach. Consuming juices with meals dilutes the stomach's natural digestive acids. For optimal digestion and absorption, drink juice alone. It's also great to have juice first thing in the morning to support natural detoxification.

• When juicing greens, wrap the leaves around harder produce. Leafy greens are not the easiest thing for a juicer to juice. The best way to extract juice from them is to roll them into a cylinder or roll them around juicier, harder produce like apples, pears, and carrots.

• Clean your juicer immediately after juicing. This might seem obvious, but it's often hard to do. Most people get so excited to drink their delicious juice that the juicer goes unattended. This creates a sticky residue that is hard to remove later.

• Drink your juice soon after juicing it. It's optimal to drink your juice within 20 minutes of juicing. Juice is fragile and spoils quickly. Once you prepare your drink, it starts losing nutrients and will oxidize over time. Ideally, you'll want to drink it within 8 hours of making it. Masticating juicers use a slow juicing process that preserves nutrients better, and the juice will keep for up to 36 hours. Check your juicer manual for how long you can store your juice.

• Save time by prepping produce. Are you in a time crunch? Prep your vegetables ahead of time and store them in the fridge. I don't recommend doing this more than 2 days in advance because produce has a tendency to dry out. A lot of "morning juicers" like to prep produce before bed so it's ready to go at the start of the day.

• Don't waste your produce. Use leaves and stems in your juices. In most cases, leaves and stems of produce are perfectly fine to juice. Two examples are beet greens and strawberry tops. Keep a bowl in your refrigerator for the kale stems that you might not eat in your salad or the tops of celery stalks that you don't use for your vegetable platter because they don't look appetizing. When it's time to juice, bring out the bowl and throw them into the juicer with the rest of your ingredients.

• Cook with juice pulp. Using the pulp that is left behind in your juicer is a personal preference. If you choose to make meals with the pulp, you can be creative by adding it to soups, stews, burgers, jams, and sauces.

• Or compost juice pulp. Composting is a great way to dispose of and reuse your juice pulp. Juicing refuse makes nutrient-rich soil that will feed your garden or flower beds nicely.

• Don't juice hard pits. Pits from fruits like cherries, mangoes, peaches, plums, and apricots can damage your juicer, and oftentimes they contain toxic substances. Remove the stones before juicing.

• Avoid juicing apple and pear seeds. Apple and pear seeds contain small amounts of cyanide that may cause problems for people with sensitivities. Remove them prior to juicing.

• Always remove the peel from citrus fruits, except for lemons and limes. The peels of grapefruits, tangerines, and oranges contain bitter oils that are indigestible and cause digestive upset. Remove these peels before juicing. The only exceptions are lemons and limes.

• Line your pulp basket with a plastic bag for easy cleanup. Lining your pulp basket will save you a lot of time when it's time to clean up pulp in your juicer.

• Can't drink your juice right away? Store it in the refrigerator in an airtight container. Light, air, and heat can all zap nutrients, so an opaque container, such as stainless steel, is ideal. Glass containers also work well, but never use plastic. I love using Mason jars. Fill the container to the very top to prevent air from getting in. Air causes juice to oxidize and turn brown, and that means it may be toxic to drink. Typically, juices from melons, cabbage, and cruciferous vegetables do not store well. I recommend consuming these immediately or tossing leftovers.

• A little ginger goes a long way. If you've never juiced ginger before, know that it can be very strong and overpowering in a juice. Start by adding a ½-inch (1.3 cm) piece of the root and work your way up to more if you like it.

• Don't juice carrot or rhubarb greens. They are bitter and contain toxic substances. It's best to avoid them.

• Add your juice to a blender and mix it with a banana for a juice–milk shake combo. I find fresh juice extremely filling, but if you're looking for a more substantial drink, you might like to blend your juice with a banana or other fruits. This is perfectly fine to do and creates a new flavor profile. It's also a great way to consume fruits that can't be juiced, such as bananas.

• Don't add too many ingredients to your juice recipe. It's common for beginner juicers to juice several types of produce together and wonder why it doesn't taste good—and then never juice again. I believe simple juices are the best juices. Too many ingredients can easily make a funky-tasting juice that isn't appetizing.

• Remove the peels from mangoes and papayas. Mango and papaya peels contain irritants that might be harmful when consumed. They will also damage your juicer.

• Juice celery last. Celery has a tendency to clog up juicer machines. The easiest way to avoid this is to juice other produce before celery.

• Juicing is not just for cleanses. Juicing is a lifestyle. In a world full of processed food devoid of nutrition, juicing helps us fill nutritional gaps in an optimal, easily absorbable fashion. Although juice fasts are great to overcome illness and reset your body, you'll ultimately want to make it your goal to incorporate juicing into your regular diet to help you meet daily nutritional needs.

• Don't juice frozen produce. All fruits, vegetables, and greens that go into your juicer need to be fresh in order to extract their juice. You can buy frozen produce to juice, but you'll need to let it thaw before juicing. I recommend sticking to fresh produce. If there is a fruit or vegetable you'd like to consume but can't get it fresh, blend the frozen and thawed version in a smoothie for better results.

• Don't juice dried fruits. Dried fruits don't work well in juicers because they have no juice for the juicer to extract. Though you could soak them in water to hydrate them, I recommend juicing only fresh produce.

• Fruits and vegetables that have a low water content don't do well in juicers. Mangoes, leafy greens, and papayas have a low water content, while items like melons and cucumbers have a high water content and yield an abundance of juice. Just because some varieties of produce have a low water content doesn't mean you can't juice them, but it will change the consistency of the juice or not give you much juice. For best results, combine low-water-content produce with high-water-content produce.

• Buy organic if you can. Organic produce is free from harmful pesticides and GMOs, so it's best to use organic when consuming large amounts of produce, as we do in juices. As a general rule, I believe we should try to eat pure and toxin-free foods to avoid disease. If we don't take the time and money to invest in our health now, we'll be forced to do so later.

• Alternate your produce when juicing. The technique of alternating relatively soft kinds of produce with relatively dense ones can make it easier on your machine to extract the liquid and to yield the most juice. For example, alternating between softer things like berries and denser produce like carrots will help the juicing process. Alternating harder and softer produce is especially helpful if you own an inexpensive centrifugal juicer. In recipes where this tip comes in handy, I reference it.

Juicing for Health: An Apples-to-Zucchini Guide to the Top 30 Ingredients to Juice

While I'm fond of all fruits, vegetables, and herbs in nature, there are some that stand out head and shoulders above the rest for juicing. Here's a list of my favorites to juice and why. Put them at the top of your list when shopping for your juice kitchen or experimenting with your own recipes.

• Apples. Apples are an essential fruit for juicing. They add a light sweetness that can soften stronger vegetable blends, and they combine beautifully with most fruits and vegetables.

Apples contain pectin, which can help the body sweep away toxins and aid in the digestion of fats. They cleanse the digestive system, boost immunity, and can help reduce cholesterol. Sometimes I specify red or green; if not, any apple will do.

Apples add a light sweetness that can soften stronger vegetable blends, but they combine beautifully well with most fruits and vegetables.

• Beets. Beets have a unique, but pleasant, taste in juices. They are strong liver cleansers and a good source of iron. Beets are beneficial for building red blood cells. I occasionally specify either red or golden beets because the strong color and flavor of beets can affect how the juice tastes and how attractive the juice looks.

• Bell peppers. Bell peppers are high in silicon, which is needed for strong hair, skin, and nails. Bell peppers add a pleasantly sweet flavor to juices.

• Broccoli. Broccoli is a cruciferous vegetable. The flavor is strong, but the benefits are too important to be missed. Broccoli is high in calcium and vitamin C and helps to prevent cancer and regulate blood sugar.

• Cabbage. Cabbage juice is not the most appetizing, but it has many health benefits. It's great for helping to heal ulcers or relieve constipation, and it has wonderful cleansing properties. It can be made palatable by combining it with other juices, like carrot, that will overpower its flavor.

• Carrots. Carrots are very high in beta-carotene. They are consumed by many to help prevent cancer, boost immunity, battle infections, give you glowing skin, and ward off macular degeneration. They assist in eliminating bacteria in the colon and parasites. Carrot juice has been used for centuries to help heal many health ailments naturally, as it has a combination of elements that nourish the entire system. Some have claimed that the carrot juice molecule is like the blood molecule and that this explains why so many people have found the juice beneficial.

• Celery. Celery makes a great base in most juices and has a light salty flavor. It is high in potassium, helps to eliminate excess sodium in the body, and is detoxifying. Celery may help to normalize body temperature and calm nerves.

• Cranberries. Tart cranberries are best combined with sweeter fruits. They prevent bacteria from building up in the bladder, prostate, and kidneys. They contain mannose, which keeps the urinary tract free from infection. They also can help prevent kidney stones.

• Cucumbers. Cucumbers yield a lot of juice and provide a neutral base for any blend. They are cleansing, hydrating, and detoxifying and are a natural diuretic. They are often consumed as an aid in regulating blood pressure.

• Fennel. Fennel is aromatic and adds a unique licorice-like flavor to juices. It is a beneficial blood builder and good for women with menstrual disorders.

• Ginger. Gingerroot adds a spicy flavor and heat to any juice blend. It helps to hide strong flavors of other juices and is fantastic for preventing nausea and aiding digestion.

• Grapes. Grapes are high in antioxidants, including resveratrol, which helps fight against free radicals, and they are anti-inflammatory.

They yield a lot of juice and make a great sweet base for many juices. Sometimes I specify red or green grapes, but if not, use whatever grapes you like or have on hand.

• Grapefruits. Grapefruits offer a pleasantly sour juice that can easily be sweetened up with the addition of other produce. They are a juicy fruit, so they give a good bang for your buck. They are high in enzymes that help to burn fat and speed up metabolism. Grapefruits contain salicylic acid, which may help break down the inorganic calcium that can build up in joints and cause arthritis.

Grapefruits contain salicylic acid, which may help break down the inorganic calcium that can build up in joints and cause arthritis.

• Green beans. Green beans don't yield a lot of juice, but they help to regulate the pancreas and benefit those with blood sugar issues, including diabetics. They pair well with carrots.

• Kale. Kale is a hearty green that juices well. It is a powerhouse of nutrition, high in protein, iron, and vitamins K, A, and C, as well as in antioxidants. Kale is highly anti-inflammatory and provides excellent cardiovascular support.

• Lemons. Lemons are powerful cleansers and detoxifiers. They are high in vitamin C and highly alkalizing to the body. Lemons have powerful antibacterial properties, stimulate the liver, and increase stimulation of the bowels. They easily hide strong flavors in juices and help to curb appetites.

• Oranges. Oranges are a juicy fruit that lend a wonderful flavor to any juice. They are a good source of vitamins C and A and potassium. Oranges are alkalizing to the body and help protect against viral infections.

• Parsley. Parsley is high in chlorophyll and when added to juices will help spike natural energy and cleanse heavy metals from the body. Mixed with carrot juice, it's beneficial for problems related to the eyes. Use either flat-leaf or curly parsley, as you prefer.

• Pears. Pears add a great flavor base to any juice. They help sweep away toxins in the body and are often consumed to reduce cholesterol. Pears are a diuretic and also can have a mild laxative effect.

• Pineapples. Pineapples yield a lot of sweet, flavorful juice that combines well with a variety of produce. They are high in bromelain, which supports the entire digestive system. They help fight inflammation in the body and are often beneficial to those who have chronic pain.

• Romaine lettuce. Romaine is a great leafy green for juicing because of its delicate flavor profile. It combines well in almost any fruit or vegetable juice. Romaine is high in potas-

sium and natural sodium. It's beneficial for those with adrenal problems.

• Spinach. Spinach is a favorite leafy green for juices because of its light green taste that doesn't overpower a juice blend. It's a great choice for green juice beginners. Spinach juice is an excellent cleanser for the entire digestive tract.

• Strawberries. Although strawberries don't yield a lot of juice, they have an irresistible sweet flavor and are packed with antioxidants to fight free radicals. They are full of lycopene, which may help prevent cancer, and are good for the cardiovascular system.

• Sweet potatoes. These root vegetables are underrated. They have double the nutrition of white potatoes and are power-packed with nutrients like beta-carotene. They also have vitamin D, iron, potassium, and magnesium. The flavor of sweet potatoes is fabulous when juiced, but pure sweet potato juice can be thick, and it is rarely drunk alone. The juice is easily made palatable by pairing it with higher-water-content produce.

• Swiss chard. Swiss chard has a strong flavor and therefore needs to be mixed with other produce when juicing. It's abundant in nutrients that make it beneficial for blood sugar issues, bone health, and eye health.

Swiss chard is abundant in nutrients that make it beneficial for blood sugar issues, bone health, and eye health.

• Tomatoes. Tomatoes yield a good amount of juice and contribute toward many tasty vegetable-juice combinations. Tomato juice is rich in calcium, sodium, potassium, and magnesium. It's also rich in the antioxidant lycopene, which is said to protect the body against various cancers.

• Turmeric. Turmeric root is a great addition to any juice. It has long been known to have several useful medicinal properties, including aiding digestive health. It contains volatile oils with anti-inflammatory properties.

• Watermelon. Watermelon is highly hydrating and cleansing. It is a natural diuretic and has anticoagulant properties. Watermelon's sweet juice is addictive.

• Wheatgrass. Wheatgrass is an edible grass grown from wheat berry seeds. It can be juiced with your juices or in a shot by itself. While you don't need to consume much wheatgrass to gain its benefits, it doesn't yield much juice, and you need a special juicer to extract it. Wheatgrass is used to heal a wide range of ailments. Studies have shown that its nutrient profile builds red blood cell count, detoxifies, extends energy, and repairs DNA.

• Zucchini. Zucchini is fabulous for juicing. It provides a wonderful light base for any juice and is a great substitute for cucumbers. Nutritionally, zucchini supports cardiovascular health by helping to lower cholesterol.

VEGETABLES

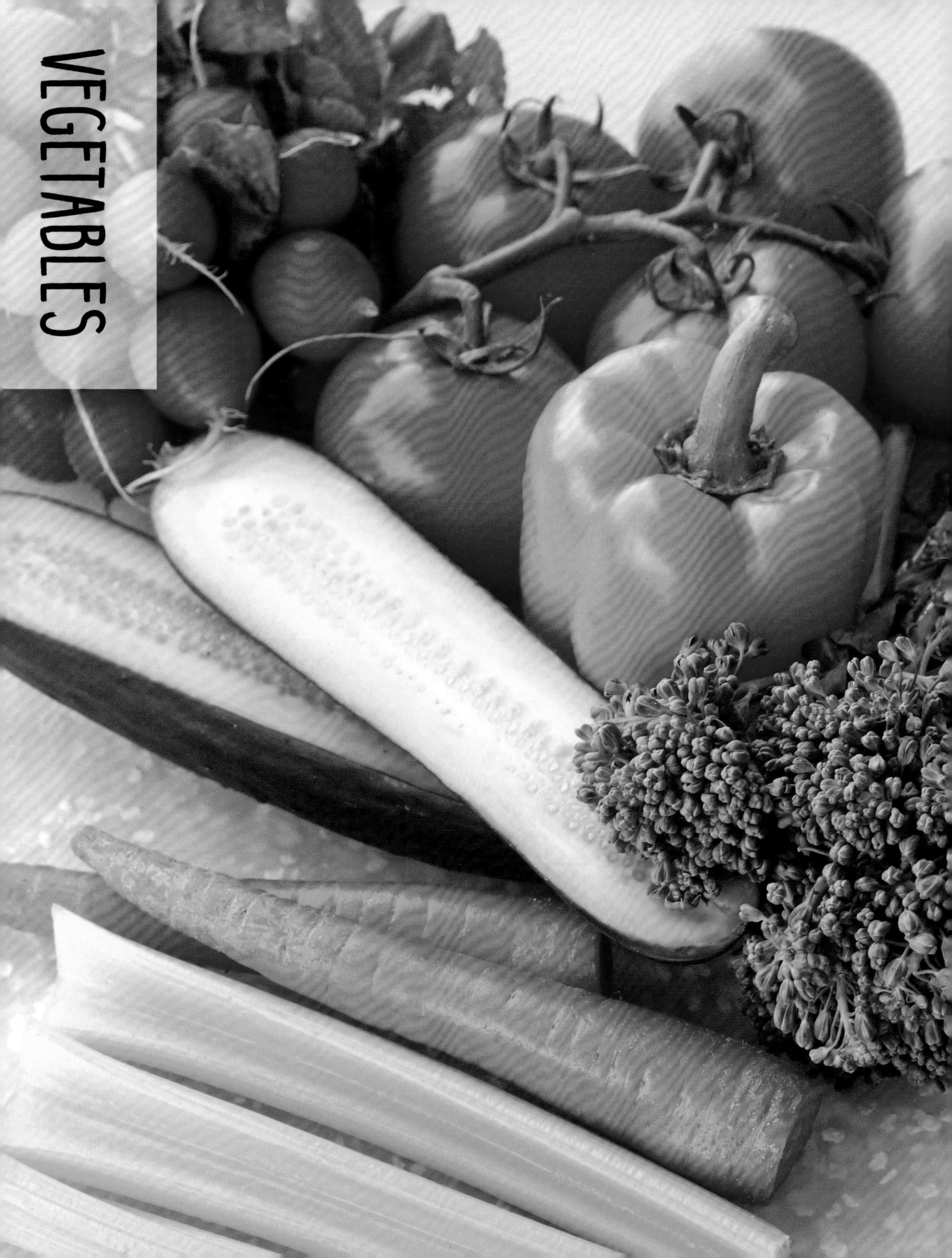

VEGETABLE
JUICES

Vegetable juices can be really tasty. They definitely don't all taste like canned tomato juice, and most combinations have a nice balance between sweet and savory. You'll be surprised how some vegetables taste in juice and how well they combine together to make tasty drinks. Take time to find a go-to vegetable juice that you like and can make often. It's the easiest, fastest way to get nutrition from vegetables you might not eat daily. Your body will thank you.

◀ Carrot Crush

Makes 12 to 16 ounces (355 to 475 ml)

This is a common go-to juice for many people. Carrots will be your new love in this crisp, clean juice.

> 2 apples
> 1 lemon
> 8 carrots

1. Core the apples and cut them into slices. Cut the peel off of the lemon and cut it in half.

2. Juice the apples, lemon, and carrots together. Serve immediately.

🥕 **JUICY TIP**
Make sure you are using fresh, large carrots for your juices. The "baby" carrots sold in a bag will not yield much juice and typically have been rinsed in a water-chlorine solution.

Veg Royale

Makes 12 to 16 ounces (355 to 475 ml)

I love giving this juice to family members and friends who have sinus issues. Radishes may help reduce inflammation in this area and help to clear out mucus.

> 2 tomatoes
> 1 radish
> 1 handful of spinach leaves
> 7 carrots
> 1 celery stalk

1. Cut the tomatoes into quarters.

2. Juice the tomatoes, radish, spinach, carrots, and celery together, alternating the different kinds of produce as you juice (see page 23). Serve immediately.

Veggie Starlet ▶

Makes 12 to 16 ounces (355 to 475 ml)

Get the glow from the inside out with this skin-nourishing combination.

> 2 apples
> 1 beet
> 4 carrots
> 2 celery stalks
> 4 sprigs of fresh parsley

1. Core the apples and cut them into slices. Cut the beet into quarters.

2. Juice the apples, beet, carrots, celery, and parsley together, alternating the different kinds of produce as you juice (see page 23). Serve immediately.

Orange Zing

Makes 12 to 16 ounces (355 to 475 ml)

Get ready to be surprised. Tomatoes and oranges are lovely together in this juice.

   4 oranges
   2 tomatoes
   4 celery stalks

1. Cut the peels off of the oranges. Slice the tomatoes into wedges.

2. Juice the oranges, tomatoes, and celery together. Serve immediately.

☞ **JUICY TIP**
Celery's organic sodium, potassium, and other electrolytes make it the perfect ingredient for a post-workout rehydration and recovery drink. Its nutrients help replenish the electrolytes you lose while exercising.

Energy Cocktail

Makes 12 to 16 ounces (355 to 475 ml)

Pump up the energy with this tasty juice combination.

   ½ of a white potato
   2 apples
   8 carrots
   1 small handful of fresh parsley

1. Cut the potato half into spears. Core the apples and cut them into slices.

2. Juice the potato, apples, carrots, and parsley together, alternating the different kinds of produce as you juice (see page 23). Serve immediately.

Cayenne Kicker

Makes 12 to 16 ounces (355 to 475 ml)

You'll feel the heat as you kick back this delightful veggie juice. Cayenne is anti-inflammatory and supports the cardiovascular system.

> 3 tomatoes
> 1 red or orange bell pepper
> 3 celery stalks
> Pinch of cayenne pepper

1. Cut the tomatoes into quarters. Cut the stem off of the bell pepper and cut it into strips.

2. Juice the tomatoes, bell pepper, and celery together. Pour into a glass and add a pinch of cayenne pepper. Serve immediately.

Beet Sunrise ▶

Makes 12 to 16 ounces (355 to 475 ml)

What a great way to start the day! Cleanse and nourish with this tasty drink.

> 1 beet
> 1 lemon
> ½ of a cucumber
> 5 carrots

1. Cut the beet into quarters. Leave the peel on the lemon and cut it in half. Cut the cucumber half into spears.

2. Juice the beet, lemon, cucumber, and carrots together. Serve immediately.

Cucumber-ade

Makes 12 to 16 ounces (355 to 475 ml)

This juice will hydrate and cleanse from the inside out.

> 2 cucumbers
> 1 lemon
> 1 lime
> 1-inch (2.5 cm) piece of fresh ginger

1. Cut the cucumbers into spears. Cut the peels off of the lemon and lime and cut them in half.

2. Juice the cucumbers, lemon, lime, and ginger together. Serve immediately.

◀ Ginger Mixer

Makes 12 to 16 ounces (355 to 475 ml)

This is a classic go-to veggie juice. I've never met anyone who didn't like it.

> 3 apples
> 7 carrots
> 1-inch (2.5 cm) piece of fresh ginger

1. Core the apples and cut them into slices.

2. Juice the apples, carrots, and ginger together. Serve immediately.

Asparagus Ace

Makes 12 to 16 ounces (355 to 475 ml)

Yes, asparagus can taste good in juice! The carrots and celery help to balance out the assertive flavor of the asparagus.

> 8 carrots
> 3 asparagus stalks
> 2 celery stalks

1. Juice the carrots, asparagus, and celery together, alternating the different kinds of produce as you juice (see page 23). Serve immediately.

Sweet Potato Sunshine

Makes 12 to 16 ounces (355 to 475 ml)

Sweet potatoes and carrots are great for glowing, radiant skin. If you have a problem with blemishes, try this combination.

> 2 sweet potatoes
> 6 carrots

1. Cut the sweet potatoes into long spears.

2. Juice the sweet potatoes and carrots together. Serve immediately.

Beet Slinger ▶

Makes 12 to 16 ounces (355 to 475 ml)

If you've never had beet juice, try it in this sweet and decadent juice.

1 beet
3 apples
6 large carrots

1. Cut the beet into quarters. Core the apples and cut them into slices.

2. Juice the beet, apples, and carrots together. Serve immediately.

Veg Crush

Makes 12 to 16 ounces (355 to 475 ml)

Would you love to eat carrots, bell peppers, broccoli, and parsley all in one sitting but you are not sure how to make them taste good? This juice is your answer!

> 1 red bell pepper
> 8 carrots
> 2 broccoli florets
> 3 sprigs of fresh parsley

1. Cut the stem off of the bell pepper and cut it into strips.

2. Juice the bell pepper, carrots, broccoli, and parsley together, alternating the different kinds of produce as you juice (see page 23). Serve immediately.

👍 JUICY TIP

Red, orange, and yellow bell peppers are surprisingly sweet and yummy in juices. Use them in place of sweet fruit to sweeten your vegetable juices. Most varieties of green bell peppers, however, are not very sweet.

Flaming Fennel

Makes 12 to 16 ounces (355 to 475 ml)

Fennel has a unique flavor that blends quite nicely with pears, apples, and beets.

> 3 apples
> 1 pear
> 1 medium fennel bulb
> 1 beet with greens (greens optional)

1. Core the apples and pear and cut them into slices. Slice the fennel bulb into wedges. Cut the beet into quarters.

2. Juice the apples, pear, fennel, and beet together. Juice a few of the beet greens, too, if you'd like. Serve immediately.

Pineapple Dawn

Makes 12 to 16 ounces (355 to 475 ml)

This really should be called heaven in a glass. I absolutely love this blend.

> 1 apple
> 5 large carrots
> 1 cup (165 g) fresh pineapple chunks
> 4 celery stalks

1. Core the apple and cut it into slices.

2. Juice the apple, carrots, pineapple, and celery together. Serve immediately.

V6 Juice

Makes 12 to 16 ounces (355 to 475 ml)

If you're into red vegetable juices from the supermarket, you will love this combination. Whenever I start drinking this, I can't stop.

> 4 large tomatoes
> 1 beet
> 4 carrots
> 5 celery stalks
> 1 small handful of spinach leaves
> 1 small bunch of fresh parsley

1. Cut the tomatoes into quarters. Cut the beet into quarters.

2. Juice the tomatoes, beet, carrots, celery, spinach, and parsley together, alternating the different kinds of produce as you juice (see page 23). Serve immediately.

Red Pepper Plush ▶

Makes 12 to 16 ounces (355 to 475 ml)

If you're typically a tomato juice fan, this one is for you. The sweet bell peppers and carrots help to balance the acidity of tomatoes nicely. Add the chile pepper if you like a little heat in your juices.

> 2 red bell peppers
> 1 tomato
> 1 red cayenne or Fresno chile pepper (optional)
> 4 carrots

1. Cut the stems off of the bell peppers and cut them into strips. Slice the tomato into wedges. If you're going to juice the chile pepper, remove the seeds and stem.

2. Juice the bell peppers, tomato, chile pepper (if you are using it), and carrots together. Serve immediately.

Veggie-tini

Makes 12 to 16 ounces (355 to 475 ml)

The sweetness of pineapple balances out the kale and parsley in this anti-inflammatory drink.

> 3 kale leaves
> 10 large carrots
> 1 cup (165 g) fresh pineapple chunks
> 2 sprigs of fresh parsley

1. Juice the kale, carrots, pineapple, and parsley together, alternating the different kinds of produce as you juice (see page 23). Serve immediately.

Carrot Dandy

Makes 12 to 16 ounces (355 to 475 ml)

This recipe took some tweaking, but I think it's just right. Cauliflower is definitely not often found in your typical vegetable juices, but it's worthy of a juice because its health benefits are strong.

> ½ of a zucchini
> ½ of a lemon
> 2 cups (200 g) cauliflower florets
> 7 large carrots

1. Cut the zucchini half into spears. Leave the peel on the lemon half.

2. Juice the zucchini, lemon, cauliflower, and carrots together, alternating the different kinds of produce as you juice (see page 23). Serve immediately.

◀ Tomato Tonic

Makes 12 to 16 ounces (355 to 475 ml)

If you're feeling a little under the weather or need some natural antibiotic power, this is the juice for you.

4 medium tomatoes
5 celery stalks
1 garlic clove

1. Cut the tomatoes into quarters.

2. Juice the tomatoes, celery, and garlic together. Serve immediately.

☞ **JUICY TIP**
Garlic is highly antibacterial and anti-inflammatory. Only juice one clove at a time to avoid overpowering your juices.

◀ Veggie Tonic

Makes 12 to 16 ounces (355 to 475 ml)

This juice tastes good with a little seasoning. Try adding a few drops of a bottled hot sauce or some sea salt and freshly ground black pepper to spice it up.

> 1 cucumber
> 1 large tomato
> ½ of a lime
> 4 celery stalks

1. Cut the cucumber into spears. Slice the tomato into wedges. Leave the peel on the lime half.

2. Juice the cucumber, tomato, lime, and celery together. Serve immediately.

☞ **JUICY TIP**
If you prefer savory-tasting drinks, add extra celery to your vegetable juices to add a naturally salty flavor.

Parsnip Parfait

Makes 12 to 16 ounces (355 to 475 ml)

Parsnips and carrots are a traditional combination for helping you to obtain silky, smooth skin.

> 4 parsnips
> 6 large carrots

1. Juice the parsnips and carrots together. Serve immediately.

🍎 **JUICY TIP**
If the parsnip taste is too strong for you in this or any other juice recipe, add 1 cored and sliced apple to balance the flavors.

Garden Glow

Makes 12 to 16 ounces (355 to 475 ml)

This tasty juice successfully mellows out the flavor of the calcium-rich broccoli.

> 1 apple
> 1 medium cucumber
> 1 cup (71 g) broccoli florets
> 2 large carrots
> 2 large celery stalks

1. Core the apple and cut it into slices. Cut the cucumber into spears.

2. Juice the apple, cucumber, broccoli, carrots, and celery together. Serve immediately.

Scarlet Night

Makes 12 to 16 ounces (355 to 475 ml)

This juice is perfect for days when you need to recover from some poor diet choices you might recently have made. It's high in lycopene, vitamin A, potassium, and magnesium.

> 4 tomatoes
> 1 parsnip
> 2 large carrots
> 3 celery stalks

1. Cut the tomatoes into quarters.

2. Juice the tomatoes, parsnip, carrots, and celery together. Serve immediately.

Ruby Slumber

Makes 12 to 16 ounces (355 to 475 ml)

This low-sugar beet juice is health in a glass. If you love sweet beet juice, you'll enjoy this drink.

> 2 red beets
> ½ of an apple
> 4 celery stalks
> 2 kale leaves

1. Cut the beets into quarters. Core the apple half and cut into slices.

2. Juice the beets, apple, celery, and kale together, alternating the different kinds of produce as you juice (see page 23). Serve immediately.

Red Warrior

Makes 12 to 16 ounces (355 to 475 ml)

This juice is strong and mighty, with all the nutrients you need for a workout or a long day ahead. I like to make this on a busy day when I need to focus.

>   1 beet
>   1 apple
>   1 cucumber
>   3 large carrots
>   1 celery stalk
>   1 small bunch of wheatgrass (optional)

1. Cut the beet into quarters. Core the apple and cut it into slices. Cut the cucumber into spears.

2. Juice the beet, apple, cucumber, carrots, celery, and wheatgrass together, alternating the different kinds of produce as you juice (see page 23). Serve immediately.

☞ JUICY TIP

A small bunch of wheatgrass can add a strong nutritional punch to any fruit, vegetable, or green juice. If you plan on juicing wheatgrass often, invest in a wheatgrass juicer or a masticating juicer to extract the maximum amount of juice from the grass.

Golden Sunset

Makes 12 to 16 ounces (355 to 475 ml)

This sunny juice is bursting with flavor and nutrients.

>   1 apple
>   5 carrots
>   1 handful of spinach leaves
>   3 celery stalks

1. Core the apple and cut it into slices.

2. Juice the apple, carrots, spinach, and celery together, alternating the different kinds of produce as you juice (see page 23). Serve immediately.

Green Glory

Makes 12 to 16 ounces (355 to 475 ml)

Brussels sprouts are not everyone's favorite vegetable. This blend is so delicious that you'll barely notice they're in the drink.

    2 apples
    1 lime
    3 brussels sprouts
    3 celery stalks

1. Core the apples and cut them into slices. Cut the lime in half, leaving the peel on.

2. Juice the apples, lime, brussels sprouts, and celery together. Serve immediately.

Red Cadillac

Makes 12 to 16 ounces (355 to 475 ml)

This unlikely blend is chock-full of skin-loving nutrients and is high in beta-carotene.

    1 sweet potato
    1 red bell pepper
    6 carrots

1. Cut the sweet potato into spears. Cut the stem off of the bell pepper and cut it into strips.

2. Juice the sweet potato, bell pepper, and carrots together. Serve immediately.

Purple Daisy ▶

Makes 12 to 16 ounces (355 to 475 ml)

If you want to benefit from the stomach-soothing properties of cabbage, this juice is for you.

    2 pears
    ½ of a lemon
    2 carrots
    2 purple cabbage leaves

1. Core the pears and cut them into slices. Leave the peel on the lemon half.

2. Juice the pears, lemon, carrots, and cabbage together, alternating the different kinds of produce as you juice (see page 23). Serve immediately.

GREEN
JUICES

Most people know that greens are good for you and that adding them to your diet has numerous health benefits. Yet most people don't want to have a bowl of spinach salad for breakfast, especially when it's 6 a.m. and they're heading out the door to start the day. Is this you? Green juices to the rescue! I believe green juices should be at the top of everyone's list as staple juices in a healthy diet. Green juices include a portion of leafy green vegetables, which contain high doses of blood-building chlorophyll. Green juices also help to alkalize the pH balance in your body and rebuild red blood cells, resulting in sky-high energy, healthy detoxing, and increased well-being.

Green Swizzle

Makes 12 to 16 ounces (355 to 475 ml)

This is one of my favorite go-to green juices. You won't even taste the spinach in this tasty drink.

>   2 pears
>   1 large apple
>   2 cups (60 g) spinach leaves
>   2 celery stalks

1. Core the pears and apple and cut them into slices.

2. Juice the pears, apple, spinach, and celery together, alternating the different kinds of produce as you juice (see page 23). Serve immediately.

Mint-ade

Makes 12 to 16 ounces (355 to 475 ml)

If the refreshing taste of mint is at the top of your list, you're going to love this sweet-plus-tart combination.

>   4 green apples
>   2 limes
>   6 fresh mint leaves
>   2 romaine lettuce leaves

1. Core the apples and cut them into slices. Cut the peels off of the limes and cut them in half.

2. Juice the apples, limes, mint leaves, and romaine lettuce together, alternating the different kinds of produce as you juice (see page 23). Serve immediately.

☞ **JUICY TIP**
Mint is a digestive and will help settle an uneasy stomach.

Green Goddess ▶

Makes 12 to 16 ounces (355 to 475 ml)

This green juice is for anyone wanting a glow from the inside out, just like a goddess. It's low in sugar, has two types of greens, and is super hydrating.

> 1 large cucumber
> 1 apple
> 1 cup (67 g) kale leaves
> 1 cup (47 g) romaine lettuce leaves
> 3 celery stalks
> 1 cup (235 ml) coconut water

1. Cut the cucumber into spears. Core the apple and cut it into slices.

2. Juice the cucumber, apple, kale, romaine lettuce, and celery together, alternating the different kinds of produce as you juice (see page 23).

3. Add the coconut water to the juice and stir gently to combine. Serve immediately.

🥥 JUICY TIP
To leave sweet fruit out of a green juice recipe, add coconut water to the drink to lighten it and sweeten up the flavor.

Citrus Crush

Makes 12 to 16 ounces (355 to 475 ml)

Apples and oranges combine beautifully in this juice to temper the strong flavor of the kale. If you're new to green juicing, try this one first.

> 4 apples
> 2 oranges
> 4 handfuls of kale leaves

1. Core the apples and cut them into slices. Peel the oranges and slice them into wedges.

2. Juice the apples, oranges, and kale together, alternating the different kinds of produce as you juice (see page 23). Serve immediately.

🍊 JUICY TIP

Wrap green leaves around other fruits and veggies before feeding them into the juicing chute. It helps prevent juicer clogs and ensures you get the most liquid out of leafy greens.

Broccoli Balancer

Makes 12 to 16 ounces (355 to 475 ml)

Broccoli isn't always my favorite vegetable to juice, but this produce combination is at the top of my list. You might find yourself juicing this one often, as I do.

> 3 pears
> 5 celery stalks
> 3 broccoli florets
> 1 handful of romaine lettuce leaves

1. Core the pears and cut them into slices.

2. Juice the pears, celery, broccoli, and romaine lettuce together, alternating the different kinds of produce as you juice (see page 23). Serve immediately.

Kale Aces

Makes 12 to 16 ounces (355 to 475 ml)

I simply love how the carrots, pineapple, and cranberries mix in this juice. No one will ever guess kale is in it.

> 1 apple
> 2 fresh pineapple spears
> 10 large carrots
> 1 cup (100 g) cranberries
> 1 handful of kale leaves

1. Core the apple and cut it into slices.

2. Juice the apple, pineapple, carrots, cranberries, and kale together, alternating the different kinds of produce as you juice (see page 23). Serve immediately.

Green Cider ▶

Makes 12 to 16 ounces (355 to 475 ml)

If you're looking for an easy go-to green juice that you can make every day, make this the one. It's tasty and combines three nutrient-dense ingredients that will do any body good.

> 4 green apples
> 5 celery stalks
> 5 romaine lettuce leaves

1. Core the apples and cut them into slices.

2. Juice the apples, celery, and romaine lettuce together, alternating the different kinds of produce as you juice (see page 23). Serve immediately.

Pineapple Flip

Makes 12 to 16 ounces (355 to 475 ml)

Whenever I have leftover watercress from my salads, I make sure to use it in this juice. It's simple but really tasty.

½ of a fresh pineapple
1 handful of watercress

1. Cut the pineapple half into spears, leaving the rind if you like.

2. Juice the pineapple and watercress together, alternating the two kinds of produce as you juice (see page 23). Serve immediately.

Kale Quencher

Makes 12 to 16 ounces (355 to 475 ml)

I love combining lime and ginger together in green juices. You'll find that the combination imparts a bit of heat and a bit of tartness to make a tasty, healthful juice.

3 apples
½ of a lime
1 cup (67 g) kale leaves
5 celery stalks
1-inch (2.5 cm) piece of fresh ginger

1. Core the apples and cut them into slices. Cut the peel off of the lime half.

2. Juice the apples, lime, kale, celery, and ginger together, alternating the different kinds of produce as you juice (see page 23). Serve immediately.

JUICY TIP
Limes and lemons help mask the taste of strong greens in juices.

Emerald Energizer

Makes 12 to 16 ounces (355 to 475 ml)

Get ready to spring into action with this energizing recipe.

    10 carrots
    7 celery stalks
    6 sprigs of fresh parsley

1. Juice the carrots, celery, and parsley together, alternating the different kinds of produce as you juice (see page 23). Serve immediately.

☞ **JUICY TIP**
Parsley has properties that can energize your body. Drink this juice midafternoon instead of coffee for a pick-me-up.

Red Reviver

Makes 12 to 16 ounces (355 to 475 ml)

If you've had a long, hard day, turn to Red Reviver. It is filled with well-balanced nutrients to nourish your blood and support healing.

    4 apples
    2 red beets
    1 small cucumber
    1 handful of spinach leaves

1. Core the apples and cut them into slices. Cut the beets into quarters. Cut the cucumber into spears.

2. Juice the apples, beets, cucumber, and spinach together, alternating the different kinds of produce as you juice (see page 23). Serve immediately.

◄ Jade Oasis

Makes 12 to 16 ounces (355 to 475 ml)

You will be in green juice heaven with this drink! I make this on hot summer days when I want a sweet, refreshing green juice.

> 1 cucumber
> 2 cups (300 g) green grapes
> 2 cups (40 g) arugula

1. Cut the cucumber into spears.

2. Juice the cucumber, grapes, and arugula together, alternating the different kinds of produce as you juice (see page 23). Serve immediately.

🍇 JUICY TIP
Grapes blend beautifully with greens in juices and provide extra antioxidants to help your body fight off free radicals.

Cucumber Dawn

Makes 12 to 16 ounces (355 to 475 ml)

Cucumbers and greens together in a juice is one of the best ways to start your day. Try this in the morning to get hydration and a wide range of nutrients.

> 1 cucumber
> 2 apples
> 1 lemon
> 2 cups (94 g) romaine lettuce leaves
> 1-inch (2.5 cm) piece of fresh ginger

1. Cut the cucumber into spears. Core the apples and cut them into slices. Cut the peel off of the lemon and cut it in half.

2. Juice the cucumber, apples, lemon, romaine lettuce, and ginger together, alternating the different kinds of produce as you juice (see page 23). Serve immediately.

Ginger Hot Spot

Makes 12 to 16 ounces (355 to 475 ml)

Cabbage and lettuce don't sound like they'd be great together, but don't be scared; the combination tastes better than you think. Bonus: This one is good for digestion.

> 2 pears
> 1 apple
> 4 romaine lettuce leaves
> 4 green cabbage leaves
> ½-inch (1.3 cm) piece of fresh ginger

1. Core the pears and apple and cut them into slices.

2. Juice the pears, apple, romaine lettuce, cabbage, and ginger together, alternating the different kinds of produce as you juice (see page 23). Serve immediately.

☞ **JUICY TIP**
Ginger helps to neutralize the strong taste of greens in a juice.

Chard Booster

Makes 12 to 16 ounces (355 to 475 ml)

Have you had your eye on chard at your farmer's market but were not sure what to do with it? Juice it. It tastes better than you think.

> 2 large sweet potatoes
> 1 small orange
> 15 strawberries
> 2 large Swiss chard leaves

1. Cut the sweet potatoes into spears. Cut the peel off of the orange and slice it into wedges.

2. Juice the sweet potatoes, orange, strawberries, and Swiss chard together, alternating the different kinds of produce as you juice (see page 23). Serve immediately.

◀ Chard Angel

Makes 12 to 16 ounces (355 to 475 ml)

This is a dynamite blend of nutrients in a glass. You won't believe how good it tastes.

> 1 zucchini
> 1 small cucumber
> 1 small apple
> 5 strawberries
> 2 Swiss chard leaves

1. Cut the zucchini and cucumber into spears. Core the apple and cut it into slices.

2. Juice the zucchini, cucumber, apple, strawberries, and Swiss chard together, alternating the different kinds of produce as you juice (see page 23). Serve immediately.

☞ **JUICY TIP**
If the taste of green juice is challenging for you to love, start out with recipes that use lighter greens, such as romaine or butter lettuce leaves.

Beet-ade

Makes 12 to 16 ounces (355 to 475 ml)

You probably never thought you'd like beet greens. Never say never until after you try this!

- 1 large zucchini
- 3 apples
- 1 beet with stems and greens (about 2 cups, 75 g, stems and greens)

1. Cut the zucchini into spears. Core the apples and cut them into slices. Cut the beet into quarters and the stems and greens into 4-inch (10 cm) pieces.

2. Juice the zucchini, apples, beet, and stems and greens together, alternating the different kinds of produce as you juice (see page 23). Serve immediately.

🌰 JUICY TIP
Beet greens are extremely high in nutrients and chlorophyll. Don't toss them. Juice them!

Green Daisy

Makes 12 to 16 ounces (355 to 475 ml)

Do you have a bunch of leafy greens in your fridge? Try this combo. Grapefruit and pear taste delicious together.

- 1 pear
- 1 large grapefruit
- 3 celery stalks
- 1 bunch of green lettuce leaves

1. Core the pear and cut it into slices. Cut the peel off of the grapefruit and slice it into wedges.

2. Juice the pear, grapefruit, celery, and lettuce leaves together, alternating the different kinds of produce as you juice (see page 23). Serve immediately.

Broccoli Breeze

Makes 12 to 16 ounces (355 to 475 ml)

This juice is chock-full of calcium and vitamin A. It's great for strong bones.

> 3 apples
> 2 parsnips
> 1 broccoli stalk or 6 broccoli florets
> 1 large carrot
> 1 large romaine lettuce leaf

1. Core the apples and cut them into slices.

2. Juice the apples, parsnips, broccoli, carrot, and romaine lettuce together, alternating the different kinds of produce as you juice (see page 23). Serve immediately.

🥦 JUICY TIP

Broccoli can quickly overpower the flavors in a juice. Start with a small quantity and add more if desired, stopping the machine to sample the juice.

Zucchini Zing

Makes 12 to 16 ounces (355 to 475 ml)

This is an awesome recipe for anyone new to green juice. It's sweet, flavorful, and packed with nutrients.

> 2 zucchini
> 1 apple
> 2 large kale leaves
> 1 large fresh pineapple spear

1. Cut the zucchini into spears. Core the apple and cut it into slices.

2. Juice the zucchini, apple, kale, and pineapple together, alternating the different kinds of produce as you juice (see page 23). Serve immediately.

Green Royale ▶

Makes 12 to 16 ounces (355 to 475 ml)

Let this sweet citrus juice fill your cup on a
day when you need a little sun in your life.

> ½ of a cucumber
> 2 large oranges
> 1 nectarine
> 3 kale leaves

1. Cut the cucumber half into spears. Cut the
peels off of the oranges and slice them into
wedges. Pit the nectarine and cut it into slices.

2. Juice the cucumber, oranges, nectarine, and
kale together, alternating the different kinds
of produce as you juice (see page 23). Serve
immediately.

Green Remedy

Makes 12 to 16 ounces (355 to 475 ml)

I more or less randomly made this juice one morning, thinking it would taste terrible. To my surprise, it didn't. The seemingly unlikely combination of produce will shock you—in a good way—once you taste it.

> 3 grapefruits
> 4 celery stalks
> 2 cups (60 g) spinach leaves

1. Cut the peels off of the grapefruits and slice them into wedges.

2. Juice the grapefruits, celery, and spinach together, alternating the different kinds of produce as you juice (see page 23). Serve immediately.

Cherry Power

Makes 12 to 16 ounces (355 to 475 ml)

Cherries are one of my favorite fruits. When you pair them with arugula in juice, it's heavenly.

> 2 apples
> 1 cucumber
> 1 cup (155 g) cherries
> 2 cups (40 g) arugula

1. Core the apples and cut them into slices. Cut the cucumber into spears. Pit the cherries.

2. Juice the apples, cucumber, cherries, and arugula together, alternating the different kinds of produce as you juice (see page 23). Serve immediately.

☞ **JUICY TIP**
If you don't have arugula, watercress is a great substitute.

Sweet Sunrise

Makes 12 to 16 ounces (355 to 475 ml)

This is one of my all-time favorite green juices. You won't detect the greens.

> 1 sweet potato
> 7 carrots
> 1 cup (165 g) fresh pineapple chunks
> 1 cup (30 g) spinach leaves

1. Cut the sweet potato into spears.

2. Juice the sweet potato, carrots, pineapple, and spinach together, alternating the different kinds of produce as you juice (see page 23). Serve immediately.

Green Limeade ▶

Makes 12 to 16 ounces (355 to 475 ml)

This lemon-lime version of green juice will make you a green juice lover if you aren't one already. Serve this one to friends.

> 1 large green apple
> 1 large lemon
> 1 lime
> 5 kale leaves
> 5 celery stalks

1. Core the apple and cut it into slices. Cut the peel off of the lemon and cut it in half. Cut the lime in half, leaving the peel on.

2. Juice the apple, lemon, lime, kale, and celery together, alternating the different kinds of produce as you juice (see page 23). Serve immediately.

Green Apple Twist ▷

Makes 12 to 16 ounces (355 to 475 ml)

This spin on green apple juice will make your taste buds sing. Feel free to make it even greener by adding more lettuce.

3 large green apples
1 cucumber
1 celery stalk
3 romaine lettuce leaves

1. Core the apples and cut them into slices. Cut the cucumber into spears.

2. Juice the apples, cucumber, celery, and romaine lettuce together, alternating the different kinds of produce as you juice (see page 23). Serve immediately.

Green Slammer

Makes 12 to 16 ounces (355 to 475 ml)

Herbs are greens, too! Cilantro adds an interesting flavor and special nutrients to this tasty juice.

- 1 zucchini
- 1 cucumber
- 1 lime
- 1 large apple
- 1 cup (30 g) spinach leaves
- 1 small handful of fresh cilantro

1. Cut the zucchini and cucumber into spears. Cut the peel off of the lime and cut it in half. Core the apple and cut it into slices.

2. Juice the zucchini, cucumber, lime, apple, spinach, and cilantro together, alternating the different kinds of produce as you juice (see page 23). Serve immediately.

☞ **JUICY TIP**
When experimenting with your own green juice recipes, remember that zucchini is a great juice "base" in green drinks.

Mango Fusion

Makes 12 to 16 ounces (355 to 475 ml)

It took me a long time to figure out just how to combine mangoes in a green juice. This one hits the spot.

- 1 large zucchini
- 1 mango
- ½ of a lime
- 1 celery stalk
- 2 cups (40 g) arugula

1. Cut the zucchini into spears. Cut the peel off of the mango and discard the pit. Cut the flesh into spears or chunks. Leave the peel on the lime half.

2. Juice the zucchini, mango, lime, celery, and arugula together, alternating the different kinds of produce as you juice (see page 23). Serve immediately.

Green Craze

Makes 12 to 16 ounces (355 to 475 ml)

If you're up for a little twist on your typical green juices, this spicy combo will energize your whole body. I love it at midday for a pick-me-up.

    1 apple
    1 large cucumber
    1 lime
    1 cup (67 g) kale leaves
    4 broccoli florets
    ½-inch (1.3 cm) piece of fresh ginger
    ½-inch (1.3 cm) piece of fresh turmeric

1. Core the apple and cut it into slices. Cut the cucumber into spears. Cut the lime in half, leaving the peel on.

2. Juice the apple, cucumber, lime, kale, broccoli, ginger, and turmeric together, alternating the different kinds of produce as you juice (see page 23). Serve immediately.

☞ **JUICY TIP**
Mixing turmeric and ginger together in a juice makes for a very anti-inflammatory cocktail.

Kiwi Smash ▶

Makes 12 to 16 ounces (355 to 475 ml)

Kiwis are very high in vitamin C and add a pleasant flavor to this juice. Drink this juice for cardiovascular protection and immune support.

    3 kiwifruits
    2 apples
    ½ of a cucumber
    5 celery stalks
    1 handful of spinach leaves

1. Peel the kiwis and cut them in half. Core the apples and cut them into slices. Cut the cucumber half into spears.

2. Juice the kiwi, apples, cucumber, celery, and spinach together, alternating the different kinds of produce as you juice (see page 23). Serve immediately.

HERBAL
JUICES

Herbs in your garden aren't just for your plate. They are terrific juice enhancers. Some are refreshing and some are earthy, but all of them are fragrant and medicinal in nature. Herbs can enhance your juice in a way that fruits and vegetables by themselves cannot. There's nothing like the fresh taste that mint imparts or the way that basil spices up your palate. Use them in your juices to enhance both flavor and nutritional benefits.

Strawberry Basil Blush

Makes 12 to 16 ounces (355 to 475 ml)

Basil has a spicy, unique flavor that tickles your taste buds. A little goes a long way with basil, so juice only a little until you know whether you'll like it. I think you'll love it mixed with berries and apples. I especially like this served over ice.

> 2 red apples
> 15 strawberries
> ½ of a lime
> 4 fresh basil leaves

1. Core the apples and cut them into slices.

2. Juice the apples, strawberries, lime (peel on), and basil together, alternating the different kinds of produce as you juice (see page 23). Serve immediately.

☞ **JUICY TIP**
Basil may be beneficial for lactating mothers who need to increase breast milk.

Basil Buzz

Makes 12 to 16 ounces (355 to 475 ml)

I bet you never thought basil could give you a buzz! This refreshing juice will blow you away.

> 2 apples
> 1 cucumber
> 1 lemon
> 3 fresh basil leaves

1. Core the apples and cut them into slices. Cut the cucumber into spears. Cut the peel off of the lemon and cut it in half.

2. Juice the apples, cucumber, lemon, and basil together, alternating the different kinds of produce as you juice (see page 23). Serve immediately.

Mint Melody

Makes 12 to 16 ounces (355 to 475 ml)

Freshen from the inside out with this cooling sweet treat.

3 cups (495 g) fresh pineapple chunks
2 celery stalks
8 sprigs of fresh mint

1. Juice the pineapple, celery, and mint together, alternating the different kinds of produce as you juice (see page 23). Serve immediately.

☞ **JUICY TIP**
Fresh mint helps to naturally freshen breath. Skip the breath mints and juice it instead!

Cilantro Crush

Makes 12 to 16 ounces (355 to 475 ml)

Cilantro helps to remove heavy metal toxins from your body, and it imparts a fresh taste to juices.

1 medium white potato
1 small apple
6 carrots
1 small bunch of fresh cilantro

1. Cut the potato into spears. Core the apple and cut it into slices.

2. Juice the potato, apple, carrots, and cilantro together, alternating the different kinds of produce as you juice (see page 23). Serve immediately.

Oregano Oasis

Makes 12 to 16 ounces (355 to 475 ml)

Do you have some oregano growing in your garden? Use it in this flavorful juice.

1 beet
8 carrots
A few sprigs of fresh oregano

1. Cut the beet into quarters.

2. Juice the beet, carrots, and oregano together. Serve immediately.

> ☞ **JUICY TIP**
> When juicing most herbs, a little goes a long way. They are potent both medicinally and in flavor.

Sage Sunrise ▷

Makes 12 to 16 ounces (355 to 475 ml)

Sage is not just for cooking. It's great in juices, too; its flavor is subtle. Sage contains a variety of antioxidants in the form of volatile oils, flavonoids, and phenolic acids.

1 pear
7 medium carrots
1 small bunch of fresh sage sprigs
1-inch (2.5 cm) piece of fresh ginger

1. Core the pear and cut it into slices.

2. Juice the pear, carrots, sage, and ginger together, alternating the different kinds of produce as you juice (see page 23). Serve immediately.

> ☞ **JUICY TIP**
> Sage is an outstanding memory enhancer and helps promote better brain function. It has been used in the treatment of cerebrovascular disease for over a thousand years.

Thyme Toddy ▶

Makes 12 to 16 ounces (355 to 475 ml)

Thyme adds a delightful punch to this classic juice. This herb is often used medicinally to stop coughing, fight acne, and lower blood pressure and cholesterol.

4 apples
2 celery stalks
½ cup (19 g) chopped fresh thyme

1. Core the apples and cut them into slices.

2. Juice the apples, celery, and thyme together, alternating the different kinds of produce as you juice (see page 23). Serve immediately.

Kiwi Mint-ade

Makes 12 to 16 ounces (355 to 475 ml)

This thick, refreshing combination is sure to freshen your breath and give you a burst of energy.

> 3 kiwifruits
> 2 cups (330 g) fresh pineapple chunks
> 3 celery stalks
> 1 cup (96 g) chopped fresh mint

1. Peel the kiwis and cut them in half.

2. Juice the kiwi, pineapple, celery, and mint together, alternating the different kinds of produce as you juice (see page 23). Serve immediately.

Fruity Parsley Punch

Makes 12 to 16 ounces (355 to 475 ml)

I've found that parsley pairs nicely with fresh fruit juices, and this recipe is no exception. This punch has an earthy taste and won't be for everyone, but if you're up for a change of pace, try this one out.

> 2 oranges
> 1 mango
> 3 carrots
> ½ cup (30 g) chopped fresh parsley

1. Cut the peels off of the oranges and slice them into wedges. Cut the peel off of the mango and discard the pit. Cut the flesh into spears or chunks.

2. Juice the oranges, mango, carrots, and parsley together, alternating the different kinds of produce as you juice (see page 23). Serve immediately.

Cilantro Cooler

Makes 12 to 16 ounces (355 to 475 ml)

The addition of coconut water in this juice makes it a low-sugar blend and also gives it a hydrating boost.

> 1 large cucumber
> 1 lemon
> 1 large bunch of fresh cilantro
> 1 cup (235 ml) coconut water

1. Cut the cucumber into spears. Cut the peel off of the lemon and cut it in half.

2. Juice the cucumber, lemon, and cilantro together, alternating the different kinds of produce as you juice (see page 23).

3. Add the coconut water to the juice and stir gently to combine. Serve immediately.

Carrot Rosemary Cocktail

Makes 12 to 16 ounces (355 to 475 ml)

Rosemary has been used medicinally for calming tension. This yummy juice might just help relieve a stress headache.

> 2 apples
> 1 pear
> 6 carrots
> 2 sprigs of fresh rosemary

1. Core the apples and cut them into slices. Core the pear and cut it into slices.

2. Juice the apples, pear, carrots, and rosemary together, alternating the different kinds of produce as you juice (see page 23). Serve immediately.

◀ Green Julep

Makes 12 to 16 ounces (355 to 475 ml)

Ease your digestive system with the mint in this limy green juice.

> 2 apples
> 1 lime
> 3 celery stalks
> 1 head of romaine lettuce
> 7 sprigs of fresh mint

1. Core the apples and cut them into slices. Cut the peel off of the lime and cut it in half.

2. Juice the apples, lime, celery, romaine lettuce, and mint together, alternating the different kinds of produce as you juice (see page 23). Serve immediately.

Parsley Plush ▶

Makes 12 to 16 ounces (355 to 475 ml)

This sweet, fruity juice is good for cleansing
and for combating inflammation.

> 1 pear
> 2 cups (330 g) fresh pineapple chunks
> 4 romaine lettuce leaves
> 1 cup (60 g) fresh parsley

1. Core the pear and cut it into slices.

2. Juice the pear, pineapple, romaine lettuce,
and parsley together, alternating the different
kinds of produce as you juice (see page 23).
Serve immediately.

Rosemary Slammer

Makes 12 to 16 ounces (355 to 475 ml)

Rosemary is a stunningly flavorful addition to this classic juice. A little goes a long way with this herb.

 2 apples
 1 pear
 1 beet
 3 celery stalks
 1 sprig of fresh rosemary

1. Core the apples and cut them into slices. Core the pear and cut it into slices. Cut the beet into quarters.

2. Juice the apples, pear, beet, celery, and rosemary together, alternating the different kinds of produce as you juice (see page 23). Serve immediately.

Tarragon Cocktail

Makes 12 to 16 ounces (355 to 475 ml)

This tarragon-infused carrot juice is bursting with flavor.

 7 carrots
 1 cup (165 g) fresh pineapple chunks
 1 small bunch of fresh tarragon

1. Juice the carrots, pineapple, and tarragon together, alternating the different kinds of produce as you juice (see page 23). Serve immediately.

◀ Dill Angel

Makes 12 to 16 ounces (355 to 475 ml)

These surprising flavors combine to create an amazing flavor profile.

> 3 green apples
> 1 medium cucumber
> 1 small bunch of fresh dill

1. Core the apples and cut them into slices. Cut the cucumber into spears.

2. Juice the apples, cucumber, and dill together, alternating the different kinds of produce as you juice (see page 23). Serve immediately.

☞ **JUICY TIP**
Always use fresh herbs for juicing. Dried herbs will not yield any juice.

Minty Green Cocktail

Makes 12 to 16 ounces (355 to 475 ml)

If mint is your thing, and green juices are your favorite, this cocktail is perfect for you.

> 2 pears
> 1 lime
> ½ of a cucumber
> 2 cups (60 g) spinach leaves
> 5 sprigs of fresh mint

1. Core the pears and cut them into slices. Cut the peel off of the lime and cut it in half. Cut the cucumber half into spears.

2. Juice the pears, lime, cucumber, spinach, and mint together, alternating the different kinds of produce as you juice (see page 23). Serve immediately.

Tarragon Lemon-ale

Makes 12 to 16 ounces (355 to 475 ml)

This spiced-up lemonade with tarragon is a hit every time.

  2 lemons
  2 apples
  1 pear
  1 small bunch of fresh tarragon

1. Cut the peels off of the lemons. Core the apples and cut them into slices. Core the pear and cut it into slices.

2. Juice the lemons, apples, pear, and tarragon together, alternating the different kinds of produce as you juice (see page 23). Serve immediately.

Cilantro Celery Punch

Makes 12 to 16 ounces (355 to 475 ml)

Celery helps balance out the strong flavor of the cilantro in this juice and makes the drink extremely detoxifying.

  1 lemon
  2 cups (300 g) green grapes
  6 celery stalks
  1 bunch of fresh cilantro
  1-inch (2.5 cm) piece of fresh ginger

1. Cut the peel off of the lemon and cut it in half.

2. Juice the lemon, grapes, celery, cilantro, and ginger together, alternating the different kinds of produce as you juice (see page 23). Serve immediately.

◀ Oregano Royale

Makes 12 to 16 ounces (355 to 475 ml)

Oregano is highly antibacterial, and when you add it to fresh juice, you have a powerful health tonic. If you're into savory juices, you'll love the almost pizza-like flavor of this one.

2 apples
1 red or yellow bell pepper
2 kale leaves
2 celery stalks
3 sprigs of fresh oregano

1. Core the apples and cut them into slices. Cut the stem off of the bell pepper and cut it into strips.

2. Juice the apples, bell pepper, kale, celery, and oregano together, alternating the different kinds of produce as you juice (see page 23). Serve immediately.

☞ **JUICY TIP**
Marjoram is a milder, sweeter, and more delicate version of its close cousin, oregano. Feel free to use marjoram in place of oregano in your juice recipes.

Parsley Lemonade

Makes 12 to 16 ounces (355 to 475 ml)

Do you think you don't like parsley? This green juice will change your mind.

2 lemons
2 pears
1 large cucumber
2 cups (120 g) fresh parsley

1. Cut the peels off of the lemons and cut them in half. Core the pears and cut them into slices. Cut the cucumber into spears.

2. Juice the lemons, pears, cucumber, and parsley together, alternating the different kinds of produce as you juice (see page 23). Serve immediately.

Sage Booster

Makes 12 to 16 ounces (355 to 475 ml)

Sage is often used medicinally to treat sore throats and coughs.

2 pears
1 lime
1 small wedge of green cabbage
5 celery stalks
1 bunch of fresh sage leaves

1. Core the pears and cut them into slices. Cut the peel off of the lime and cut it in half.

2. Juice the pears, lime, cabbage, celery, and sage together, alternating the different kinds of produce as you juice (see page 23). Serve immediately.

☞ **JUICY TIP**
Sage is a good source of vitamin K, which is important for bones and healthy blood clotting. Sage also contains calcium, potassium, and beta-carotene.

Sweet Thyme Rosemary Punch

Makes 12 to 16 ounces (355 to 475 ml)

Mixing thyme and rosemary in this pink punch makes for a fabulous way to start the day.

  2 oranges
  1 lemon
  1 beet
  2 sprigs of fresh thyme
  1 sprig of fresh rosemary

1. Cut the peels off of the oranges and lemon and slice them into wedges. Cut the beet into quarters.

2. Juice the oranges, lemon, beet, thyme, and rosemary together, alternating the different kinds of produce as you juice (see page 23). Serve immediately.

Dill Daisy

Makes 12 to 16 ounces (355 to 475 ml)

Dill has been used as a headache and hiccup remedy since ancient times. Keep this savory juice in mind should you need it.

  1 cucumber
  1 tomato
  1 lemon
  4 carrots
  1 cup (30 g) spinach leaves
  1 bunch of fresh dill

1. Cut the cucumber into spears. Slice the tomato into wedges. Cut the peel off of the lemon and cut it in half.

2. Juice the cucumber, tomato, lemon, carrots, spinach, and dill together, alternating the different kinds of produce as you juice (see page 23). Serve immediately.

Spearmint Sour

Makes 12 to 16 ounces (355 to 475 ml)

This limeade blend is fresh and fantastic!
Serve this one over ice.

> 3 apples
> 2 limes
> 5 celery stalks
> 4 sprigs of fresh spearmint

1. Core the apples and cut them into slices.
Cut the peels off of the limes and cut them
in half.

2. Juice the apples, limes, celery, and
spearmint together, alternating the different
kinds of produce as you juice (see page 23).
Serve immediately.

Rosemary Watermelon Crush ▶

Makes 12 to 16 ounces (355 to 475 ml)

If any juice had a wow factor, it would be
this one. The complex flavors blend together
beautifully for a healthful, refreshing juice.

> 2 kiwifruits
> 2 cups (300 g) watermelon chunks
> 4 strawberries
> 1 sprig of fresh rosemary

1. Peel the kiwis and cut them in half.

2. Juice the kiwis, watermelon, strawberries,
and rosemary together, alternating the
different kinds of produce as you juice (see
page 23). Serve immediately.

Pineapple Spearmint Cooler

Makes 12 to 16 ounces (355 to 475 ml)

Nothing goes better with pineapple than spearmint! This is perfect for a hot day.

> 2 cups (330 g) fresh pineapple chunks
> 5 celery stalks
> 4 sprigs of fresh spearmint

1. Juice the pineapple, celery, and spearmint together, alternating the different kinds of produce as you juice (see page 23). Serve immediately over ice.

Rosemary Grapefruit Guzzler

Makes 12 to 16 ounces (355 to 475 ml)

A little bit of rosemary goes a long way in juice. This sweet, sour, and herbal combo is perfect for brunch parties.

> 2 large grapefruits
> 1 apple
> 2 sprigs of fresh rosemary

1. Cut the peels off of the grapefruits and slice them into wedges. Core the apple and cut it into slices.

2. Juice the grapefruits, apple, and rosemary together, alternating the different kinds of produce as you juice (see page 23). Serve immediately.

Thyme Pineapple Juice

Makes 12 to 16 ounces (355 to 475 ml)

The perfume-like aroma that the thyme imparts to this juice is amazing.

> 1 cup (165 g) fresh pineapple chunks
> 1 cup (150 g) grapes
> 5 carrots
> 3 sprigs of fresh thyme

1. Juice the pineapple, grapes, carrots, and thyme together, alternating the different kinds of produce as you juice (see page 23). Serve immediately.

☞ **JUICY TIP**

Woody herbs like thyme can be juiced without being stripped from the stem. Just toss the whole sprigs into your juicer the same way you would other produce, alternating the different kinds of hard and soft ingredients as you juice.

Herb Heaven

Makes 12 to 16 ounces (355 to 475 ml)

This well-rounded herbal green juice is fragrant and highly detoxifying.

> 2 apples
> 1 pear
> 1 cucumber
> 5 carrots
> 1 bunch of fresh cilantro
> 1 bunch of fresh parsley
> Small handful of fresh sage leaves

1. Core the apples and cut them into slices. Core the pear and cut it into slices. Cut the cucumber into spears.

2. Juice the apples, pear, cucumber, carrots, cilantro, parsley, and sage together, alternating the different kinds of produce as you juice (see page 23). Serve immediately.

FRUIT
JUICES

Fruit juices are everyone's favorite juices. They are sweet and refreshing, and drinking a glass is like having dessert. If you're looking to benefit from the health-promoting properties of fruit as you enjoy a sweet, sinful-like taste, then fruit juices are for you. One glass is a great way to curb cake and cookie cravings. Fruits typically have a high amount of antioxidant compounds, which contribute toward heart health and are anti-aging. While you won't want to consume fruit-only juices all day every day, there is certainly room for them in a healthy, balanced diet. Enjoy these sweet drinks!

Pear Plush

Makes 12 to 16 ounces (355 to 475 ml)

Yes, this classic juice is quite sweet, but don't let that fool you. It's packed with nutrients to nourish your whole body. I have no doubt you'll love it.

> 4 pears
> 3 apples

1. Core the pears and apples and cut them into slices.

2. Juice the pears and apples together. Serve immediately.

🍐 JUICY TIP

Many fruit juices taste refreshing on the rocks. Pour your juice over ice for a cooling treat.

Pink Melon-ade

Makes 12 to 16 ounces (355 to 475 ml)

This beautiful rose-colored drink tastes like a cool summer morning.

> 3 cups (480 g) cantaloupe chunks
> 10 strawberries

1. Juice the cantaloupe and strawberries together. Serve immediately.

Cranberry Crush

Makes 12 to 16 ounces (355 to 475 ml)

Cranberries support a healthy urinary tract. In this juice, the sweet pears balance out the sourness of the cranberries very well.

> 2 pears
> 2 cups (200 g) cranberries

1. Core the pears and cut them into slices.

2. Juice the pears and cranberries together, alternating the two kinds of produce as you juice (see page 23). Serve immediately.

Yellow Sling

Makes 12 to 16 ounces (355 to 475 ml)

I know this combination might sound weird, but it's wildly good.

    1 medium yellow bell pepper
    3 cups (495 g) fresh pineapple chunks

1. Cut the stem off of the bell pepper and cut it into strips.

2. Juice the bell pepper and pineapple together, alternating the two kinds of produce as you juice (see page 23). Serve immediately.

Rose Punch

Makes 12 to 16 ounces (355 to 475 ml)

This fruity combination is just perfect for a morning brunch. Serve this over ice.

    3 apples
    1 orange
    10 strawberries

1. Core the apples and cut them into slices. Cut the peel off of the orange and slice it into wedges.

2. Juice the orange, apples, and strawberries together, alternating the different kinds of produce as you juice (see page 23). Serve immediately.

❀ JUICY TIP

Juicing the green tops of the strawberries is fine. They have beneficial nutrients, too, including being high in vitamin C, and are often used in tea. Strawberry leaves are traditionally used to promote digestion and relieve joint pain.

Citrus Royale

Makes 12 to 16 ounces (355 to 475 ml)

This amazing combination uses a sweet potato, an unexpected ingredient in a juice, and gives it a tropical twist.

1 orange
1 sweet potato
2 cups (330 g) fresh pineapple chunks

1. Cut the peel off of the orange and slice it into wedges. Cut the sweet potato into spears.

2. Juice the orange, sweet potato, and pineapple together. Serve immediately.

Raspberry Rambler

Makes 12 to 16 ounces (355 to 475 ml)

Raspberries don't yield much juice, but they add a fabulous flavor. Try them in this fan favorite. The fresh ginger adds a little zing, too.

2 apples
4 carrots
1 cup (125 g) raspberries
1-inch (2.5 cm) piece of fresh ginger

1. Core the apples and cut them into slices.

2. Juice the apples, carrots, raspberries, and ginger together, alternating the different kinds of produce as you juice (see page 23). Serve immediately.

Pink Zing ▶

Makes 12 to 16 ounces (355 to 475 ml)

This juice is your go-to light refreshment for a hot day.

   1 large lemon
   2 cups (300 g) watermelon chunks

1. Slice the lemon into wedges, leaving the peel on.

2. Juice the lemon and watermelon together. Serve immediately.

Cantaloupe Blush

Makes 12 to 16 ounces (355 to 475 ml)

This amazing juice is common in South America. Pineapple and cantaloupe make a perfect pair. Serve this over ice.

> 2 cups (330 g) fresh pineapple chunks
> 2 cups (320 g) cantaloupe chunks

1. Juice the cantaloupe and pineapple together. Serve immediately.

🍍 JUICY TIP

It's fine to juice the rinds of cantaloupes and pineapples if you have a strong juicer. Be sure to wash the rinds very well before juicing to remove any dirt or pesticides.

Peach Hurricane

Makes 12 to 16 ounces (355 to 475 ml)

This sweet dessert juice is like peach pie in a glass.

> 4 peaches
> 1 lemon
> 1 cup (150 g) red grapes

1. Pit the peaches and cut them into slices. Cut the peel off of the lemon and cut it in half.

2. Juice the peaches, lemon, and grapes together. Serve immediately.

Peach-tastic

Makes 12 to 16 ounces (355 to 475 ml)

Peaches are a good source of vitamins C and A, making them great for healthy skin. They also can calm an upset stomach.

3 peaches
1 small lime
3 celery stalks

1. Pit the peaches and cut them into slices. Cut the peel off of the lime and slice it into wedges.

2. Juice the peaches, lime, and celery together. Serve immediately.

Cranberry Apple Smash ▶

Makes 12 to 16 ounces (355 to 475 ml)

I've taken the classic cran-apple combo and sweetened it with grapes. Drink this often if you'd like to prevent chronic urinary tract infections.

3 apples
2 cups (300 g) grapes
1 cup (100 g) cranberries

1. Core the apples and cut them into slices.

2. Juice the apples, grapes, and cranberries together. Serve immediately.

🍎 JUICY TIP
Apple seeds contain trace amounts of cyanide. While it's okay to juice a few, it's best to core your apples before juicing to steer clear of these toxins.

Cherry Craze

Makes 12 to 16 ounces (355 to 475 ml)

There is no better way to juice cherries than in a pineapple-lime drink. Serve this over ice.

> 10 cherries
> 1 lime
> ½ of a fresh pineapple

1. Pit the cherries. Cut the lime in half, leaving the peel on. Cut the pineapple half into spears.

2. Juice the cherries, lime, and pineapple together. Serve immediately.

🍒 JUICY TIP
Always be sure to pit any stone fruit prior to juicing. It will seriously damage your juicer blades if you run hard pits through the machine.

Apricot Angel

Makes 12 to 16 ounces (355 to 475 ml)

Sweet apricots are high in beta-carotene, which has been shown in studies to play a positive role in cardiovascular health. Drink them up in this tasty combo.

> 6 apricots
> 1 pear
> 2 cups (300 g) green grapes

1. Pit the apricots and cut them into slices. Core the pear and cut it into slices.

2. Juice the apricots, pear, and grapes together. Serve immediately.

◄ Pomegranate Cider

Makes 12 to 16 ounces (355 to 475 ml)

Pomegranate has been called the fruit of the gods, and many cultures have used the fruit medicinally for centuries, especially for gastroenterological ailments. Keep the doctor away with this apple and pom cider. It's especially refreshing served over ice.

> **5 apples**
> **1 pomegranate**

1. Core the apples and cut them into slices. Cut the pomegranate in half. Remove the arils with your hands in a bowl of water. Drain the water and discard the pith and peel.

2. Juice the apples and pomegranate arils together. Serve immediately.

☞ **JUICY TIP**
Never juice the white pith of the pomegranate. It contains compounds that are toxic and may make you sick if ingested.

◄ Persimmon Twist

Makes 12 to 16 ounces (355 to 475 ml)

Persimmons, which are only available for a short season, make the most amazing juice. They add a delicate, sweet flavor to drinks that will have you coming back for more.

> 2 persimmons
> 2 oranges
> 1 apple

1. Peel the persimmons and slice them into wedges. Cut the peels off of the oranges and slice them into wedges. Core the apple and cut it into slices.

2. Juice the persimmons, oranges, and apple together. Serve immediately.

Fruit Flamer

Makes 12 to 16 ounces (355 to 475 ml)

This is one of my favorite fruit juices. It's sweet and fresh, and the lime really puts it over the top.

> 1 peach
> 1 lime
> 10 strawberries
> 2 cups (300 g) grapes

1. Pit the peach and cut it into slices. Cut the lime in half, but leave the peel on.

2. Juice the peach, lime, strawberries, and grapes together, alternating the different kinds of produce as you juice (see page 23). Serve immediately.

Grape Oasis

Makes 12 to 16 ounces (355 to 475 ml)

You'll be in heaven with this juice. It's perfectly balanced to hydrate and nourish.

> 1 lemon
> 1 cup (150 g) purple or red grapes
> 1 cup (145 g) blueberries
> 4 celery stalks
> ½-inch (1.3 cm) piece of fresh ginger

1. Cut the peel off of the lemon and cut it in half.

2. Juice the lemon, grapes, blueberries, celery, and ginger together, alternating the different kinds of produce as you juice (see page 23). Serve immediately.

Melon Zingo

Makes 12 to 16 ounces (355 to 475 ml)

I dream of this juice at the beginning of summer, when fresh fruits start to hit the markets in force.

> 1 lime
> 1 cup (160 g) cantaloupe chunks
> 1 cup (165 g) fresh pineapple chunks
> 1 cup (150 g) watermelon chunks

1. Cut the peel off of the lime and cut it in half.

2. Juice the lime, cantaloupe, pineapple, and watermelon together. Serve immediately.

◄ Waterlime Cooler

Makes 12 to 16 ounces (355 to 475 ml)

Lime-spiked watermelon is delightful any time of day. Leave the rind on the melon, if you like.

> 1 lime
> 2 cups (300 g) watermelon chunks
> ½-inch (1.3 cm) piece of fresh ginger

1. Cut the peel off of the lime and cut it in half.

2. Juice the lime, watermelon, and ginger together. Serve immediately.

🍉 JUICY TIP

Feel free to juice the rind of all watermelon varieties. The rind contains beneficial nutrients like vitamins C and B6. It also contains citrulline. The body converts citrulline to the amino acid arginine, which helps relax blood vessels and supports healthy blood pressure.

Pink Parfait

Makes 12 to 16 ounces (355 to 475 ml)

Raspberries have a sweet, thick juice that is irresistible. Don't let this one pass you by.

3 apples
1 cup (125 g) raspberries

1. Core the apples and cut them into slices.

2. Juice the apples and raspberries together, alternating the two kinds of produce as you juice (see page 23). Serve immediately.

Honeydew Sour ▶

Makes 12 to 16 ounces (355 to 475 ml)

There's something about this juice that reminds me of what you should have on a holiday getaway. It's so sweet and tropical in flavor that you can't go wrong.

½ of a honeydew melon
2 limes

1. Cut the half of the honeydew into small chunks or wedges; leave the rind on, if you like. Cut the limes in half, but leave the peel on.

2. Juice the honeydew and limes together. Serve immediately.

Apple Flip ▶

Makes 12 to 16 ounces (355 to 475 ml)

This classic blend is packed with essential nutrients to keep you fueled for the day.

   2 apples
   1 lemon
   5 carrots

1. Core the apples and cut them into slices. Cut the peel off of the lemon and cut it in half.

2. Juice the apples, lemon, and carrots together. Serve immediately.

Purple Cocktail

Makes 12 to 16 ounces (355 to 475 ml)

Most people only eat cabbage cooked, but many nutrients are lost this way. Juicing it preserves precious nutrients, including vitamin C, vitamin A, and potassium. You will barely taste the cabbage in this juice.

> 1 large orange
> ½ cup (45 g) coarsely chopped purple cabbage
> 1 cup (165 g) fresh pineapple chunks

1. Cut the peel off of the orange and slice it into wedges.

2. Juice the orange, cabbage, and pineapple together, alternating the different kinds of produce as you juice (see page 23). Serve immediately.

Blackberry Bliss

Makes 12 to 16 ounces (355 to 475 ml)

Blackberries can be a little tough to juice because of their tiny seeds, which often clog the juicer. But don't let this stop you. They produce a lovely juice.

> 2 apples
> 2 kiwifruits
> 1 pear
> 1 cup (145 g) blackberries

1. Core the apples and cut them into slices. Peel the kiwis and cut them in half. Core the pear and cut it into slices.

2. Juice the apples, kiwis, pear, and blackberries together, alternating the different kinds of produce as you juice (see page 23). Serve immediately.

Blueberry Sparkle

Makes 12 to 16 ounces (355 to 475 ml)

Blueberries are not only tasty, but are also very high in antioxidants and have been shown in studies to slow down vision loss. This juice tastes like blueberry pie. Drink up!

> 4 cups (600 g) red grapes
> 1 pint (290 g) blueberries

1. Juice the blueberries and grapes together. Serve immediately.

☞ **JUICY TIP**

In most cases, adding light leafy greens to any fruit juice recipe will taste okay. You can experiment by adding a few leaves of romaine or green leaf lettuce to your favorite juice recipe for added nutrients.

Berry Fix

Makes 12 to 16 ounces (355 to 475 ml)

When berry season is on your doorstep, make this juice. It's like drinking a mixed-berry pie.

> 2 pears
> 1 apple
> 1 cup (125 g) raspberries
> 7 strawberries

1. Core the pears and cut them into slices. Core the apple and cut it into slices.

2. Juice the pears, apple, raspberries, and strawberries together, alternating the different kinds of produce as you juice (see page 23). Serve immediately.

◀ Scarlet Sizzle

Makes 12 to 16 ounces (355 to 475 ml)

This red beauty will make you pucker and swoon at the same time. Feel free to add in some beet greens, if you like.

> **1 grapefruit**
> **1 apple**
> **1 beet**

1. Cut the peel off of the grapefruit and slice it into wedges. Core the apple and cut it into slices. Cut the beet into quarters.

2. Juice the grapefruit, apple, and beet together. Serve immediately.

◀ Orange Slumber

Makes 12 to 16 ounces (355 to 475 ml)

You'll see this classic fruit blend in juice bars across the country. It's that good.

    1 orange
    4 carrots
    2 cups (330 g) fresh pineapple chunks

1. Cut the peel off of the orange and slice it into wedges.

2. Juice the orange, carrots, and pineapple together. Serve immediately.

Papaya Dawn

Makes 12 to 16 ounces (355 to 475 ml)

Papaya is a cleansing fruit and is a great help for those with constipation and digestive problems.

    3 cups (420 g) papaya chunks
    15 strawberries

1. Juice the papaya chunks and strawberries together, alternating the two kinds of produce as you juice (see page 23). Serve immediately.

☞ **JUICY TIP**
Papaya contains papain, a beneficial digestive enzyme.

CITRUS
JUICES

Everyone loves a great glass of orange juice. But don't stop at juicing just oranges! There are many fantastic combinations that use the variety of citrus we have available. Citrus juices make the best summertime and brunch juices. They typically contain a high amount of vitamin C, along with compounds called flavonoids that help your body to fight off free radicals, which cause aging. They are good sources of folate and potassium. I know your taste buds and your body will love these.

Grapefruit Sunrise

Makes 12 to 16 ounces (355 to 475 ml)

If you'd like to drink grapefruit juice but don't like the sour flavor, this blend is calling your name. Apples take away the bitter taste nicely.

4 apples
2 grapefruits

1. Core the apples and cut them into slices. Cut the peels off of the grapefruits and slice them into wedges.

2. Juice the apples and grapefruits together. Serve immediately.

Morning Craze

Makes 12 to 16 ounces (355 to 475 ml)

This citrusy combination is the perfect juice for a late-morning brunch.

2 oranges
1 grapefruit
2 cups (290 g) strawberries

1. Cut the peels off of the oranges and grapefruit and slice them into wedges.

2. Juice the oranges, grapefruit, and strawberries together, alternating the different kinds of produce as you juice (see page 23). Serve immediately.

⊛ JUICY TIP

Try different varieties of oranges to see which ones you like better. For example, Cara Cara and blood oranges are two flavorful types you might enjoy.

Pineapple Sunshine

Makes 12 to 16 ounces (355 to 475 ml)

Who doesn't love pineapple? Lemons enhance pineapple's addictive sweetness in this blend.

> 2 lemons
> 2 cups (330 g) fresh pineapple chunks

1. Cut the peels off of the lemons and slice them into wedges.

2. Juice the lemons and pineapple together. Serve immediately.

Key Lime Cocktail ▶

Makes 12 to 16 ounces (355 to 475 ml)

This cocktail will carry you away to the Florida Keys. Yes, please.

> 2 apples
> 1 lime
> 1 lemon
> 7 key limes

1. Core the apples and cut them into slices. Remove the peel from the lime and lemon and cut them in half.

2. Juice the apples, lime, lemon, and key limes together, alternating the different kinds of produce as you juice (see page 23). Serve immediately.

🍊 JUICY TIP

It's perfectly fine to juice the rind of key limes. They add a great flavor to your juices.

Blood Orange Cocktail ▶

Makes 12 to 16 ounces (355 to 475 ml)

I am in love with the gorgeous red-purple hue of blood oranges. They are not as sweet as typical oranges and have a sharper citrus flavor.

3 blood oranges
½ cup (75 g) blackberries

1. Cut the peels off of the blood oranges and slice them into wedges.

2. Juice the oranges and blackberries together, alternating the two kinds of produce as you juice (see page 23). Serve immediately.

Spicy Citrus Sling

Makes 12 to 16 ounces (355 to 475 ml)

Turmeric and ginger are extremely anti-inflammatory. Pair them with the vitamin C in this juice and you'll be in good shape.

> 3 oranges
> 1 mango
> 1-inch (2.5 cm) piece of fresh turmeric
> 1-inch (2.5 cm) piece of fresh ginger

1. Cut the peels off of the oranges and slice them into wedges. Cut the peel off the mango and discard the pit. Cut the flesh into spears or chunks.

2. Juice the oranges, mango, turmeric, and ginger together, alternating the different kinds of produce as you juice (see page 23). Serve immediately.

Lemon Lime Ale

Makes 12 to 16 ounces (355 to 475 ml)

Sweet lemon-lime juice is perfect for midday refreshment.

> 2 apples
> 2 lemons
> 1 lime

1. Core the apples and cut them into slices. Cut the peels off of the lemons and the lime and cut them in half.

2. Juice the apple, lemons, and lime together. Serve immediately.

◀ Citrus Buzz

Makes 12 to 16 ounces (355 to 475 ml)

Get high—and healthy—on citrus fruits with this sweet-and-sour blend.

> 2 oranges
> 1 lemon
> 1 lime

1. Cut the peels off of the oranges, lemon, and lime and slice them into wedges.

2. Juice the oranges, lemon, and lime together. Serve immediately.

Spicy Orange Sunrise

Makes 12 to 16 ounces (355 to 475 ml)

Do you like your juice a little bit spicy? Ginger adds some nice heat to this classic citrus blend.

> 3 oranges
> 1 apple
> 1-inch (2.5 cm) piece of fresh ginger

1. Cut the peels off of the oranges and slice them into wedges. Core the apple and cut it into slices.

2. Juice the oranges, apple, and ginger together. Serve immediately.

☞ **JUICY TIP**
You don't need to remove the skin from ginger when juicing.

Pink Sunburst

Makes 12 to 16 ounces (355 to 475 ml)

This gorgeous pink juice is high in vitamin C. The nutrients in beets help support the functioning of the liver.

> 3 tangerines
> 1 orange
> 1 lemon
> 1 beet

1. Cut the peels off of the tangerines, orange, and lemon and slice them into wedges. Cut the beet into quarters.

2. Juice the tangerines, orange, lemon, and beet together. Serve immediately.

Golden Sun

Makes 12 to 16 ounces (355 to 475 ml)

Like beaming sunrays from the sky, this sunny juice will invigorate your entire body.

> 1 grapefruit
> 1 lime
> 1 orange
> 1-inch (2.5 cm) piece of fresh ginger

1. Cut the peels off of the grapefruit, lime, and orange and slice them into wedges.

2. Juice the grapefruit, lime, orange, and ginger together. Serve immediately.

Citrus Fusion

Makes 12 to 16 ounces (355 to 475 ml)

Golden beets complement citrus nicely and also add nutrients like iron and folate.

> 2 grapefruits
> 1 orange
> 1 golden beet

1. Cut the peel off of the grapefruits and orange and slice them into wedges. Cut the beet into quarters.

2. Juice the grapefruits, orange, and beet together. Serve immediately.

Grapefruit Guzzler

Makes 12 to 16 ounces (355 to 475 ml)

This juicy cocktail is just perfect for a day at the beach. Take this juice with you in a sealed glass mason jar packed in an ice-filled cooler. Don't forget your straw!

   2 grapefruits
   2 cups (330 g) fresh pineapple chunks

1. Cut the peels off of the grapefruits and slice them into wedges.

2. Juice the grapefruits and pineapple together. Serve immediately.

Citrus Breakfast

Makes 12 to 16 ounces (355 to 475 ml)

I just love waking up to this twist on classic orange juice.

   2 oranges
   1 lime
   1 apple

1. Cut the peels off of the oranges and lime and slice them into wedges. Core the apple and cut it into slices.

2. Juice the oranges, lime, and apple together. Serve immediately.

> **JUICY TIP**
> Cut the peel off of citrus fruits rather than peeling them with your hands. It's easier and faster.

Orange Snap ▶

Makes 12 to 16 ounces (355 to 475 ml)

What could be better than orange-pineapple juice? Not much! This fresh and sweet kid-friendly combo pleases everyone who tries it.

2 oranges
2 cups (330 g) fresh pineapple chunks

1. Cut the peels off of the oranges and slice them into wedges.

2. Juice the oranges and pineapple together. Serve immediately.

☼ JUICY TIP
Adding sparkling mineral water to any citrus juice instantly makes it a classy brunch favorite.

Sour Strawberry

Makes 12 to 16 ounces (355 to 475 ml)

This pretty-in-pink combo is packed with antioxidants.

2 grapefruits
10 strawberries

1. Cut the peels off of the grapefruits and slice them into wedges.

2. Juice the grapefruits and strawberries together, alternating the two kinds of produce as you juice (see page 23). Serve immediately.

Rose Royale

Makes 12 to 16 ounces (355 to 475 ml)

There's something about this juice that feels fancy. Pomegranate marries citrus fruits and it's divine.

2 oranges
1 lemon
1 apple
1 pomegranate

1. Cut the peels off of the oranges and lemon and slice them into wedges. Core the apple and cut it into slices. Cut the pomegranate in half. Remove the arils with your hands in a bowl of water. Drain the water and discard the pith and peel.

2. Juice the oranges, lemon, apple, and pomegranate arils together, alternating the different kinds of produce as you juice (see page 23). Serve immediately.

☞ **JUICY TIP**
Never juice the white pith of the pomegranate. It contains compounds that are toxic and may make you sick if ingested.

Berry Slammer

Makes 12 to 16 ounces (355 to 475 ml)

This is a sour juice but great if you love the strong taste of grapefruits. The blackberries add a smooth, sweet flavor.

   3 grapefruits
   1 cup (145 g) blackberries

1. Cut the peels off of the grapefruits and slice them into wedges.

2. Juice the grapefruits with the blackberries, alternating the two kinds of produce as you juice (see page 23). Serve immediately.

Citrus Zingo

Makes 12 to 16 ounces (355 to 475 ml)

If you're not sure which juice to serve your friends this weekend, this sweet-and-sour citrus blend is the one!

   1 grapefruit
   1 orange
   3 key limes
   10 strawberries

1. Cut the peels off of the grapefruit and orange and slice them into wedges. There is no need to cut the peels off of the key limes.

2. Juice the grapefruit, orange, key limes, and strawberries together, alternating the different kinds of produce as you juice (see page 23). Serve immediately.

◀ Raspberry Aces

Makes 12 to 16 ounces (355 to 475 ml)

This perfect pairing of citrus and berries is enough to make anyone fall in love with juice all over again.

2 oranges
1 grapefruit
1 cup (125 g) raspberries

1. Cut the peels off of the oranges and grapefruit and slice them into wedges.

2. Juice the oranges, grapefruit, and raspberries together, alternating the different kinds of produce as you juice (see page 23). Serve immediately.

Citrus Angel

Makes 12 to 16 ounces (355 to 475 ml)

Looking to add a little chlorophyll to your juice? Adding a bit of lettuce to a citrus juice will add nutrition without adding a "green" taste.

> 2 oranges
> 1 lemon
> 1 lime
> 3 key limes
> 2 romaine lettuce leaves

1. Cut the peels off of the oranges, lemon, and lime and slice them into wedges. There is no need to cut the peels off of the key limes.

2. Juice the oranges, lemon, lime, key limes, and romaine lettuce together, alternating the different kinds of produce as you juice (see page 23). Serve immediately.

Clementine Daisy ▶

Makes 12 to 16 ounces (355 to 475 ml)

I often think bell pepper won't taste good in a juice, until I taste the juice. This combination is amazing.

> 5 clementines
> 1 orange
> 1 red bell pepper

1. Cut the peels off of the clementines. Cut the peel off of the orange and slice it into wedges. Cut the stem off of the bell pepper and cut it into strips.

2. Juice the clementines, orange, and bell pepper together. Serve immediately.

Lemon Sunburst ▶

Makes 12 to 16 ounces (355 to 475 ml)

This juice is like a little ray of sun in your cup. It's bursting with flavor and will make you smile.

> 5 clementines
> 1 large lemon
> 8 strawberries

1. Cut the peels off of the clementines and lemon. Cut the lemon in half.

2. Juice the clementines, lemon, and strawberries together, alternating the different kinds of produce as you juice (see page 23). Serve immediately.

Orange Kiss

Makes 12 to 16 ounces (355 to 475 ml)

Even if you aren't a grapefruit fan, you might like this juice. The sweet mango balances out the sourness of the grapefruit.

2 Minneola oranges
1 grapefruit
1 mango

1. Cut the peels off of the oranges and grapefruit and slice them into wedges. Cut the peel off of the mango and discard the pit. Cut the flesh into spears or chunks.

2. Juice the oranges, grapefruit, and mango together. Serve immediately.

Mandarin Plush

Makes 12 to 16 ounces (355 to 475 ml)

I love mixing kiwi with citrus in my juices. They are a perfect pair!

3 kiwifruits
4 mandarin oranges
2 oranges
1 lime

1. Peel the kiwis and cut them in half. Cut the peels from the mandarin oranges and oranges and slice them into wedges. Cut the lime in half, but leave the peel on.

2. Juice the kiwis, mandarin oranges, oranges, and lime together. Serve immediately.

⊚ JUICY TIP
Just as with other oranges and as with grapefruits, you don't want to juice the rinds of mandarin oranges. Cut the peels off of them before juicing.

◁ Lime Pucker

Makes 12 to 16 ounces (355 to 475 ml)

Your lips might pucker with this one, but I think you'll like it.

> 2 grapefruits
> 1 pear
> 6 key limes

1. Cut the peels off of the grapefruits and slice them into wedges. Core the pear and cut it into slices. Leave the key limes unpeeled.

2. Juice the grapefruits, pear, and key limes together. Serve immediately.

Orangeberry Oasis

Makes 12 to 16 ounces (355 to 475 ml)

This sweet orange-berry drink is a perfect dessert juice.

> 2 oranges
> 1 cup (145 g) blueberries
> 1 cup (165 g) fresh pineapple chunks

1. Cut the peels off of the oranges and slice them into wedges.

2. Juice the oranges, blueberries, and pineapple together, alternating the different kinds of produce as you juice (see page 23). Serve immediately.

Lemon Meringue

Makes 12 to 16 ounces (355 to 475 ml)

Like a lemon meringue pie, this juice is sweet, sour, and delightful!

   3 lemons
   1 orange
   1 apple

1. Cut the peels off of the lemons and orange and slice them into wedges. Core the apple and cut it into slices.

2. Juice the lemons, orange, and apple together. Serve immediately.

Melon Twist

Makes 12 to 16 ounces (355 to 475 ml)

This tangy twist on citrus juice will have you crying for more when the glass is done. You'll appreciate how beautifully the orange colors blend in this juice.

   2 oranges
   2 cups (320 g) cantaloupe chunks

1. Cut the peels off of the oranges and slice them into wedges.

2. Juice the oranges and cantaloupe together. Serve immediately.

◀ # Flaming Orange

Makes 12 to 16 ounces (355 to 475 ml)

Blood oranges radiate sunshine and beauty. Combine them with the other citrus fruits in this juice for a gorgeous and tasty drink.

2 blood oranges
1 grapefruit
1 lemon

1. Cut the peels off of the blood oranges, grapefruit, and lemon and slice them into wedges.

2. Juice the oranges, grapefruit, and lemon together. Serve immediately.

TROPICAL
JUICES

Picture yourself on an island with clear blue seas and white sand beaches. The wind is blowing in your hair and the sun is beating on your back. You're sipping on an exotic drink made from amazing fruits that are sweet, fruity, and incredibly fresh.

Sometimes you need a little something to zip you away to a tropical island. I promise these drinks will do just that—all while tasting great and nourishing your body. Grab your flip-flops and a sunny juice drink. I'll see you by the water!

Ginger Sun

Makes 12 to 16 ounces (355 to 475 ml)

This super hydrating citrus blend has all the flavors you'd want on a happy, sunny day.

2 tangerines
1 lime
10 strawberries
1-inch (2.5 cm) piece of fresh ginger
1 cup (235 ml) coconut water

1. Cut the peels off of the tangerines and slice them into wedges. Cut the peel off of the lime and cut it in half.

2. Juice the tangerines, lime, strawberries, and ginger together, alternating the different kinds of produce as you juice (see page 23).

3. Add the coconut water to the juice. Stir to combine. Serve immediately.

🥥 JUICY TIP
Coconut meat can be juiced, but it won't yield much liquid. If you like the flavor of coconut in your beverages, it's best to add coconut water or coconut milk after you've juiced your produce.

Red Hurricane

Makes 12 to 16 ounces (355 to 475 ml)

Papaya is a wonderful tropical fruit that isn't easy to use in a juicer but does fine in a blender. Because this juice is thick and substantial, it's great for a snack or a meal.

2 oranges
1 mango
1 cup (155 g) cherries
1 cup (140 g) papaya chunks

1. Cut the peels off of the oranges and slice them into wedges. Cut the peel off of the mango and remove the pit. Cut the flesh into spears or chunks. Pit the cherries.

2. Juice the prepared oranges, mango, and cherries together.

3. Place the papaya chunks in a blender and add the juice you have just made.

4. Blend everything together on high speed until smooth. Serve immediately.

Caribbean Night

Makes 12 to 16 ounces (355 to 475 ml)

This sweet dessert juice is perfect for a crisp, clear summer night.

> 1 pear
> 1 orange
> 1 persimmon
> 2 cups (330 g) fresh pineapple chunks
> 2 romaine lettuce leaves

1. Core the pear and cut it into slices. Cut the peel off of the orange and slice it into wedges. Cut the flesh off of the persimmon (there is no need to peel it).

2. Juice the pear, orange, persimmon, pineapple, and romaine lettuce together, alternating the different kinds of produce as you juice (see page 23). Serve immediately.

Pineapple Bombshell ▶

Makes 12 to 16 ounces (355 to 475 ml)

This is a sweet and zesty juice, just like life would be in the tropics.

> 1 lime
> 3 cups (495 g) fresh pineapple chunks

1. Slice the lime into wedges, but leave the peel on.

2. Juice the lime and pineapple together. Serve immediately.

◀ Caipirinha Crush

Makes 12 to 16 ounces (355 to 475 ml)

The caipirinha is often called the national cocktail of Brazil. Drinking a caipirinha reminds me of my own sun-filled days on Brazilian beaches. My family would make big pitchers of lime or strawberry cachaça drinks to keep the party going. I've made my own fruit juice version, without the alcohol and white sugar, to remind me of those times. Serve this over plenty of ice.

> 2 limes
> 1 large apple
> 1 cup (235 ml) coconut water

1. Cut the peels off of the limes and cut them in half. Core the apple and cut it into slices.

2. Juice the limes and apple together.

3. Add the coconut water to the juice. Stir to combine. Serve immediately.

🥥 **JUICY TIP**
Coconut water is high in electrolytes and is incredibly hydrating. If you need to rehydrate with vitamins, add coconut water to your juices for a boost of flavor and hydration.

Exotic Oasis

Makes 12 to 16 ounces (355 to 475 ml)

My Brazilian cousins Carolina and Veronica tell me they love this refreshing, tropically inspired juice and drink it quite often.

> 1 mango
> 2 cups (330 g) fresh pineapple chunks
> 6 sprigs of fresh mint

1. Cut the peel off of the mango and discard the pit. Cut the flesh into spears or chunks.

2. Juice the mango, pineapple, and mint together, alternating the produce as you juice (see page 23). Serve immediately.

☞ **JUICY TIP**
Mangoes can be juiced, but they won't yield much liquid. Be sure to remove the pit and the peel before feeding the fruit into your juicer.

Tropic-tini ▶

Makes 12 to 16 ounces (355 to 475 ml)

Let's head to the tropics with this rich,
spicy blend.

> 3 oranges
> 1 mango
> 1-inch (2.5 cm) piece of fresh ginger

1. Cut the peels off of the oranges and slice
them into wedges. Cut the peel off of the
mango and discard the pit. Cut the flesh into
spears or chunks.

2. Juice the oranges, mango, and ginger
together. Serve immediately.

Jamaica Kiss

Makes 12 to 16 ounces (355 to 475 ml)

This decadent juice is just perfection for cooling off in the heat.

> 1 large cucumber
> 1 apple
> 1 mango
> ½-inch (1.3 cm) piece of fresh ginger

1. Cut the cucumber into spears. Core the apple and cut it into slices. Cut the peel off of the mango and discard the pit. Cut the flesh into spears or chunks.

2. Juice the cucumber, apple, mango, and ginger together. Serve immediately.

Ruby Melone

Makes 12 to 16 ounces (355 to 475 ml)

This amazing melon combination is just what you'd order on your next island vacation. Now you can make it at home.

> 1 lime
> ½ of a cantaloupe
> 1 cup (150 g) grapes

1. Cut the peel off of the lime and cut it in half. Cut the cantaloupe into chunks (you can leave the rind on if you like).

2. Juice the lime, cantaloupe, and grapes together. Serve immediately.

Beach Babe Bomber

Makes 12 to 16 ounces (355 to 475 ml)

This ultimate beach babe drink is perfect for sipping by the pool or on a hot afternoon for hydration. Serve over ice.

> 1 lemon
> 1 apple
> 1 cucumber
> 1 cup (145 g) strawberries

1. Cut the peel off of the lemon and cut it in half. Core the apple and cut it into slices. Cut the cucumber into spears.

2. Juice the lemon, apple, cucumber, and strawberries together, alternating the different kinds of produce as you juice (see page 23). Serve immediately.

Star Fruit Spritz

Makes 12 to 16 ounces (355 to 475 ml)

Fresh, ripe star fruits can be hard to find. If you have access to them, I highly recommend this sweet treat.

> 3 star fruits
> 1 cucumber
> 5 strawberries

1. Cut the star fruits into smaller slices. Cut the cucumber into spears.

2. Juice the star fruits, cucumber, and strawberries together, alternating the different kinds of produce as you juice (see page 23). Serve immediately.

Golden Breeze

Makes 12 to 16 ounces (355 to 475 ml)

This unusual combination is highly refreshing. I love it for picnics.

> 1 large lemon
> 1 handful of fresh basil
> 1 cup (235 ml) coconut water

1. Cut the peel off of the lemon and slice it into wedges.

2. Juice the lemon and basil together, alternating the two kinds of produce as you juice (see page 23).

3. Add the coconut water to the juice. Stir to combine. Serve immediately.

Mango Tango

Makes 12 to 16 ounces (355 to 475 ml)

Let's tango all the way to the dance floor with this sweet, tropical blend.

> 1 lime
> 1 mango
> ½ of a cucumber
> 2 cups (330 g) fresh pineapple chunks

1. Cut the peel off of the lime and cut it in half. Cut the peel off of the mango and discard the pit. Cut the flesh into spears or chunks. Cut the cucumber half into spears.

2. Juice the lime, mango, cucumber, and pineapple together. Serve immediately.

🍍 **JUICY TIP**
Pineapple can transform any juice into a tropical treat. You don't need much. A 1-inch-thick (2.5 cm) ring or 8 to 10 chunks will be enough to gain the taste and benefits.

◄ Getaway Cocktail

Makes 12 to 16 ounces (355 to 475 ml)

Coconut water and fruit-infused coconut drinks are very common in the tropics. Adding coconut is a great way to liven up any fruit juice blend.

1 lemon
1 cup (150 g) grapes
1 cup (235 ml) coconut water

1. Cut the peel off of the lemon and cut it in half.

2. Juice the lemon and grapes together.

3. Add the coconut water to the juice. Stir to combine. Serve immediately.

Brazilian Glow

Makes 12 to 16 ounces (355 to 475 ml)

My mom is from Brazil, and I have a lot of family there. Whenever we visit, I notice the abundance of fresh fruits and their juices at roadside stands or in everyday restaurants. It's always been in style to have fruit drinks there, and red fruits are always nearby. Serve this over ice.

> 1 cup (155 g) red cherries
> 12 strawberries
> 1 cup (235 ml) coconut water

1. Pit the cherries.

2. Juice the cherries and strawberries together.

3. Add the coconut water to the juice. Stir to combine. Serve immediately.

Bermuda Rose ▶

Makes 12 to 16 ounces (355 to 475 ml)

This rose-colored juice is perfect for a peaceful, relaxing morning.

> 2 red grapefruits
> 1 cup (160 g) cantaloupe chunks
> 1 cup (125 g) raspberries

1. Cut the peels off of the grapefruits and slice them into wedges.

2. Juice the grapefruits, cantaloupe, and raspberries together, alternating the different kinds of produce as you juice (see page 23). Serve immediately.

Bahia Cocktail

Makes 12 to 16 ounces (355 to 475 ml)

Bahia is a beautiful beach-lined state in Brazil. Bahians consume an abundance of coconut milk and tropical fruits. This juice reminds me of my vacation there.

> 1 orange, peeled
> 1 cup (165 g) fresh pineapple chunks
> 2 medium carrots
> 2 tablespoons (28 ml) coconut milk

1. Slice the orange into wedges.

2. Juice the orange, pineapple, and carrots together.

3. Add the coconut milk to the juice. Stir to combine. Serve immediately.

Pear Temptation ▶

Makes 12 to 16 ounces (355 to 475 ml)

This green broccoli juice is unexpectedly delicious with the addition of coconut water.

> 3 pears
> 1 lime
> 5 broccoli florets
> 1 cup (235 ml) coconut water

1. Core the pears and cut them into slices. Cut the peel off of the lime and cut it in half.

2. Juice the pears, lime, and broccoli together.

2. Add the coconut water to the juice. Stir to combine. Serve immediately.

Pineapple Passion

Makes 12 to 16 ounces (355 to 475 ml)

This creamy, fruity drink is sure to be among your favorites.

> 1 mango
> 1 orange
> ½ of a lime
> 2 cups (330 g) fresh pineapple chunks
> 2 tablespoons (28 ml) light coconut milk

1. Cut the peel off of the mango and discard the pit. Cut the flesh into spears or chunks. Cut the peel off of the orange and slice it into wedges. Cut the peel off of the lime half.

2. Juice the mango, orange, lime, and pineapple together.

3. Add the coconut milk to the juice. Stir to combine. Serve immediately.

🥥 JUICY TIP
If you're a fan of tropical juices, keep a can of coconut milk on hand. Adding a tablespoon (15 ml) or so to your juice will transform an ordinary juice into a creamy, luscious drink.

Daydreamer

Makes 12 to 16 ounces (355 to 475 ml)

Perfect for daydreamin', this blend will add a tropical twist to your day.

> 2 oranges
> 1 grapefruit
> 1 lemon
> 10 strawberries

1. Cut the peels off of the oranges, grapefruit, and lemon and slice them into wedges.

2. Juice the oranges, grapefruit, lemon, and strawberries together, alternating the different kinds of produce as you juice (see page 23). Serve immediately.

🥥 JUICY TIP
Tropical fruit pulp can be transformed into coconut fruit dessert balls by mixing the pulp with flaked coconut and honey. Roll them into small balls and keep them in the refrigerator for an instant snack.

Sunny Swizzle

Makes 12 to 16 ounces (355 to 475 ml)

Nothing says "bring on the sun" like this melon and pineapple blend. For even more refreshment, serve over ice.

> 2 cups (320 g) cantaloupe chunks
> 1 cup (150 g) watermelon chunks
> 1 cup (165 g) fresh pineapple chunks

1. Juice the cantaloupe, watermelon, and pineapple together. Serve immediately.

Mango Viva

Makes 12 to 16 ounces (355 to 475 ml)

The juice of mango is thick, but it lends an amazing flavor to juice blends like this one. Serve over ice.

> 2 mangoes, peeled
> 6 carrots

1. Discard the mango pit. Cut the flesh into spears or chunks.

2. Juice the mangoes and carrots together. Serve immediately.

Red Melon-tini ▶

Makes 12 to 16 ounces (355 to 475 ml)

Serve this in a martini glass garnished with mint and it'll be the hit of your party.

> 1 lemon
> 3 cups (450 g) watermelon chunks
> 3 sprigs of fresh mint

1. Cut the peel off of the lemon and cut it in half.

2. Juice the lemon, watermelon, and mint together, alternating the different kinds of produce as you juice (see page 23). Serve immediately.

Hawaiian Sun

Makes 12 to 16 ounces (355 to 475 ml)

This must-try tasty juice reminds me of sitting on the beach in Hawaii, watching a glorious sunset.

> 1 beet
> ½ of a fresh pineapple
> ½-inch (1.3 cm) piece of fresh ginger
> 2 tablespoons (28 ml) light coconut milk

1. Cut the beet into quarters. Cut the pineapple half into spears.

2. Juice the beet, pineapple, and ginger together.

3. Add the coconut milk to the juice. Stir to combine. Serve immediately.

Kiwi Divine

Makes 12 to 16 ounces (355 to 475 ml)

This beautiful kiwi blend is perfect as a dessert juice to quench your sweet tooth.

> 3 kiwifruits
> 1 green apple
> 2 cups (290 g) strawberries
> 4 celery stalks

1. Peel the kiwis and cut them into quarters. Core the apple and cut it into slices.

2. Juice the kiwis, apple, strawberries, and celery together, alternating the produce as you juice (see page 23). Serve immediately.

🍌 JUICY TIP

If you want your tropical-inspired juice to keep you full longer, pour the juice into a blender, add a banana, and blend. You'll get all the nutrition plus some fiber to keep you full.

LEMONADES

There are no powdered, artificially flavored, or fake lemonades here! Fresh lemonade is refreshing and healthful. Lemons are extremely alkalizing to the body and it's a good idea to have them often. I drink a glass of lemon water for health when I wake up each day. When I began to tire of the plain-Jane versions, but still wanted the benefits of lemons, I developed these flavorful lemonade recipes as alternatives to my regular lemon water. I know you'll love these unique and healthful spins on lemonade—without the refined sugar or artificial flavors.

Blueberry Lemonade

Makes 12 to 16 ounces (355 to 475 ml)

When blueberries are in season and you can't get enough of them, make this lemonade. Not only does it provide a strong antioxidant punch, but it's also the best summertime treat.

    1 large lemon
    1 medium apple
    1 cup (145 g) blueberries
    ½ cup (120 ml) cold water

1. Slice the lemon into wedges. Leave the peel on or remove the peel if you don't like your lemonade on the tart side. Core the apple and cut it into slices.

2. Juice the lemon, apple, and blueberries together, alternating the different kinds of produce as you juice (see page 23).

3. Mix the juice with the water. Serve immediately, over ice if desired.

> ⌂ **JUICY TIP**
> Apples add sweetness to lemonade recipes without any refined sugar. If you want an even sweeter lemonade, add more apples.

Pear Lemonade

Makes 12 to 16 ounces (355 to 475 ml)

Pears make an optimal natural sweetener for fresh lemonades. Their juice tends to be a little thicker than apples, but they taste just as amazing.

    2 medium lemons
    2 medium pears
    ½ cup (120 ml) cold water

1. Cut the peels off of the lemons and slice them into wedges. Core the pears and cut them into slices.

2. Juice the lemons and pears together.

3. Mix the juice with the water. Serve immediately, over ice if desired.

◀ Sweet Lemonade

Makes 12 to 16 ounces (355 to 475 ml)

This is my classic sweet lemonade that everyone loves—sans sugar! If you are the type who loves the tartness of lemons, leave the peels on. The essential oils in the lemon peels are good for your immune system.

2 medium lemons
2 medium apples
½ cup (120 ml) cold water

1. Slice the lemons into wedges. Leave the peel on or remove the peel if you don't like your lemonade on the tart side. Core the apples and cut them into slices.

2. Juice the apples and lemons together.

3. Mix the juice with the water. Serve immediately, over ice if desired.

Orange Lemonade ▶

Makes 12 to 16 ounces (355 to 475 ml)

If you're into citrus, this one's for you! It's tart, sweet, and perfect for brunch.

> 2 oranges
> 1 large lemon
> 1 medium apple
> ½ cup (120 ml) cold water

1. Cut the peels off of the oranges and slice them into wedges. Slice the lemon into wedges. Leave the peel on or remove it if you prefer a less tart lemonade. Core the apple and cut it into slices.

2. Juice the oranges, lemon, and apple together.

3. Mix the juice with the water. Serve immediately, over ice if desired.

Raspberry Lemonade

Makes 12 to 16 ounces (355 to 475 ml)

There is something extra special about this lemonade. I'm not sure if it's the beautiful pink color or the sinfully sweet taste. The one thing I do know is that this will always be one of my favorites.

   2 medium lemons
   2 medium apples
   1 cup (125 g) raspberries
   ½ cup (120 ml) cold water

1. Cut the peel off of the lemons and slice them into wedges. Core the apples and cut them into slices.

2. Juice the lemons, apples, and raspberries together, alternating the different kinds of produce as you juice (see page 23).

3. Mix the juice with the water. Serve immediately, over ice if desired.

🫐 JUICY TIP
Leaving the peel on the lemons will add a tartness to the juice. Removing the peel removes the tartness. Experiment with the lemon peels and make lemonades to your taste preferences.

Basil Strawberry Lemonade

Makes 12 to 16 ounces (355 to 475 ml)

Perfect for a summer picnic on a hot day, this basil and strawberry lemonade goes great with snacks or a light lunch.

   1 large lemon
   1 medium apple
   1 cup (145 g) strawberries
   ½ cup (20 g) fresh basil leaves
   ½ cup (120 ml) cold water

1. Slice the lemon into wedges. Leave the peel on or remove the peel if you want a less tart lemonade. Core the apple and cut it into slices.

2. Juice the lemon, apple, strawberries, and basil together, alternating the different kinds of produce as you juice (see page 23).

3. Mix the juice with the water. Serve immediately, over ice if desired.

☞ JUICY TIP
If you're looking to help your body detox daily, try drinking lemonades when you first wake up and on an empty stomach. Lemons stimulate the liver and encourage bowel movements.

◀ Strawberry Lemonade

Makes 12 to 16 ounces (355 to 475 ml)

The classic strawberry lemonade is not like the powdered mix you had as a kid. It's fresh, tart, and sweet. Serve this one to your friends and they won't be disappointed.

1 large lemon
1 medium apple
1 cup (145 g) strawberries
½ cup (120 ml) cold water

1. Slice the lemon into wedges. Leave the peel on or remove the peel for a less tart lemonade. Core the apple and cut it into slices.

2. Juice the lemon, apple, and strawberries together, alternating the different kinds of produce as you juice (see page 23).

3. Mix the juice with the water. Serve immediately, over ice if desired.

Raspberry Mint Lemonade

Makes 12 to 16 ounces (355 to 475 ml)

This is one of my favorite lemonades, and I think it might be a keeper for you, too. The sweet raspberries mix beautifully with the mint and tingle your tongue, making for a refreshing juice.

2 medium lemons
2 medium apples
1 cup (125 g) raspberries
5 sprigs of fresh mint
½ cup (120 ml) cold water

1. Cut the peels off of the lemons and slice them into wedges. Core the apples and cut them into slices.

2. Juice the lemons, apples, raspberries, and mint together, alternating the different kinds of produce as you juice (see page 23).

3. Mix the juice with the water. Serve immediately, over ice if desired.

> **🌰 JUICY TIP**
> When cutting the peel off of a lemon, slice the base off first and then turn it over to slice the sides. This will ensure the lemon doesn't slip from your hands while cutting.

Tangerine Peach Lemonade

Makes 12 to 16 ounces (355 to 475 ml)

Tangerine + peach = a really great lemonade flavor. I know you'll love this juice as much as I do. It's one of my favorites for an afternoon break.

> 2 peaches
> 1 large lemon
> 1 medium apple
> 1 small tangerine
> ½ cup (120 ml) cold water

1. Pit the peaches and cut them into slices. Cut the peel off of the lemon and slice it into wedges. Core the apple and cut it into slices. Peel the tangerine.

2. Juice the peaches, lemon, apple, and tangerine together.

3. Mix the juice with the water. Serve immediately, over ice if desired.

Sweet Lime Lemonade ▶

Makes 12 to 16 ounces (355 to 475 ml)

I have to confess that I like the flavor of limes more than I do lemons in juice. They have a sweetness and spark that lemons don't have. Here, I've combined them with lemon to make a punchier drink.

> 2 medium apples
> 1 medium lemon
> 1 large lime
> ½ cup (120 ml) cold water

1. Core the apples and cut them into slices. Cut off the peel of the lemon. Leave the peel on the lime. Slice the lemon and lime into wedges.

2. Juice the apples, lemon, and lime together.

3. Mix the juice with the water. Serve immediately, over ice if desired.

Watermelon Strawberry Lemonade

Makes 12 to 16 ounces (355 to 475 ml)

This pretty pink lemonade is fruity and so refreshing. Feel free to add more strawberries if you want the strawberry flavor to dominate. Also feel free to serve over ice.

> 2 medium lemons
> 1 medium apple
> 1 cup (150 g) watermelon chunks
> 5 large strawberries

1. Cut the peels off of the lemons and slice them into wedges. Core the apple and cut it into slices.

2. Juice the lemons, apple, watermelon, and strawberries together, alternating the different kinds of produce as you juice (see page 23). Serve immediately.

> 🫐 **JUICY TIP**
> Lemons are a good source of vitamin C, which helps to neutralize free radicals linked to aging and disease.

Rosemary Lemonade

Makes 12 to 16 ounces (355 to 475 ml)

I know what you're thinking—rosemary in my lemonade? Trust me, it's good. Rosemary brings out the lemon flavor and adds a nice flavor of its own. If you love rosemary in your foods, you will love this lemonade.

> 2 medium lemons
> 2 medium apples
> 2 sprigs of fresh rosemary
> ½ cup (120 ml) cold water

1. Cut the peels off of the lemons and slice them into wedges. Core the apples and cut them into slices.

2. Juice the lemons, apples, and rosemary together, alternating the different kinds of produce as you juice (see page 23).

3. Mix the juice with the water. Serve immediately, over ice if desired.

◄ Ginger Lemonade

Makes 12 to 16 ounces (355 to 475 ml)

Lemons help your liver work optimally and aid in natural detoxification. Adding ginger will boost the benefits.

> 2 medium lemons
> 2 medium apples
> 1-inch (2.5 cm) piece of fresh ginger
> ½ cup (120 ml) cold water

1. Cut the peels off of the lemons and slice them into wedges. Core the apples and cut them into slices.

2. Juice the lemons, apples, and ginger together, alternating the different kinds of produce as you juice (see page 23).

3. Mix the juice with the water. Serve immediately, over ice if desired.

🍊 JUICY TIP
Lemons have antibacterial properties. Experiments have shown that they destroy bacteria quite well.

Blackberry Mint Lemonade

Makes 12 to 16 ounces (355 to 475 ml)

Blackberry and mint add a fabulous flavor and nutritional punch to lemonade. You're going to like this one.

    1 large lemon
    1 medium apple
    1 cup (145 g) blackberries
    4 sprigs of fresh mint
    ½ cup (120 ml) cold water

1. Slice the lemon into wedges. Leave the peel on or remove the peel if you don't like your lemonade on the tart side. Core the apple and cut it into slices.

2. Juice the lemon, apple, blackberries, and mint together, alternating the different kinds of produce as you juice (see page 23).

3. Mix the juice with the water. Serve immediately, over ice if desired.

Watermelon Lemonade

Makes 12 to 16 ounces (355 to 475 ml)

Nothing else screams "summertime" better than fresh, pink watermelon. Mix it up in some lemonade and you've got yourself the most refreshing drink on the planet.

    2 medium lemons
    1 medium apple
    1 cup (150 g) watermelon chunks

1. Cut the peels off of the lemons and slice them into wedges. Core the apple and cut it into slices.

2. Juice the lemons, apple, and watermelon chunks together. Serve immediately.

Peach Lemonade

Makes 12 to 16 ounces (355 to 475 ml)

This reminds me of the drink you'd have on a sweet, hot afternoon in the South. Once you taste this, you'll be taking it with you to your front porch to relax in your favorite rocking chair.

> 2 peaches
> 2 large lemons
> 1 medium apple
> ½ cup (120 ml) cold water

1. Pit the peaches and cut them into slices. Leave the peel on 1 lemon; remove the peel from the other. Slice the lemons into wedges. Core the apple and cut it into slices.

2. Juice the peaches, lemons, and apple together.

3. Mix the juice with the water. Serve immediately, over ice if desired.

🍐 JUICY TIP

If you want even sweeter lemonade, use a pear instead of an apple to sweeten up the drink naturally.

Grapefruit Lemonade

Makes 12 to 16 ounces (355 to 475 ml)

This juice is a little tart and sour. If you love the flavor of grapefruit and sweet lemonade, this will be your new favorite. Serve over ice.

> 1 large lemon
> 1 medium grapefruit
> 1 medium apple

1. Slice the lemon into wedges. Leave the peel on or remove the peel if you like your lemonade on the less tart side. Remove the peel from the grapefruit and slice it into wedges. Core the apple and cut it into slices.

2. Juice the lemon, grapefruit, and apple together. Serve immediately.

◀ Red Beet Lemonade

Makes 12 to 16 ounces (355 to 475 ml)

This is a beautiful juice and extremely healthful, too. Beets are full of iron and antioxidants to support your body. If beets usually aren't your thing, try this and you might be surprised.

  2 medium lemons
  2 medium apples
  1 small red beet

1. Cut the peels off of the lemons and slice them into wedges. Core the apples and cut them into slices. Cut the beet into quarters.

2. Juice the lemons, apples, and beet together. Serve immediately, over ice if desired.

☞ **JUICY TIP**
Try removing citrus peels with a vegetable peeler instead of with a knife. Some people find this method easier.

Cherry Lemonade

Makes 12 to 16 ounces (355 to 475 ml)

Who can resist the flavor of fresh cherries? Cherries combine wonderfully in lemonade and make a truly beautiful and tasty juice.

  2 medium lemons
  2 medium apples
  1 cup (155 g) cherries
  ½ cup (120 ml) cold water

1. Cut the peels off of the lemons and slice them into wedges. Core the apples and cut them into slices. Pit the cherries.

2. Juice the lemons, apples, and cherries together, alternating the different kinds of produce as you juice (see page 23).

3. Mix the juice with the water. Serve immediately, over ice if desired.

Kiwi Lemonade

Makes 12 to 16 ounces (355 to 475 ml)

Kiwis are a little tart and thick in juices, but their unique flavor is quite refreshing in this lemonade variation.

> 2 medium lemons
> 2 medium apples
> 2 kiwifruits
> ½ cup (120 ml) cold water

1. Cut the peels off of the lemons and slice them into wedges. Core the apples and cut them into slices. Peel the kiwis and cut them in half.

2. Juice the lemons, apples, and kiwis together, alternating the different kinds of produce as you juice (see page 23).

3. Mix the juice with the water. Serve immediately, over ice if desired.

Green Lemonade ▶

Makes 12 to 16 ounces (355 to 475 ml)

You won't even know kale is in this recipe. This lemonade hides its greens and is great for energy and cleansing. I add some water and ice cubes and take this one to the gym for hydration during my workouts.

> 2 medium lemons
> 2 medium apples
> 2 large kale leaves

1. Cut the peels off of the lemons and slice them into wedges. Core the apples and cut them into slices.

2. Juice the lemons, apples, and kale together, alternating the different kinds of produce as you juice (see page 23). Serve immediately.

Pineapple Lemonade

Makes 12 to 16 ounces (355 to 475 ml)

Pineapple adds a tropical twist to lemonade that is irresistible. Enjoy this sweet combo.

>   2 medium lemons
>   1 medium apple
>   1 cup (165 g) fresh pineapple chunks
>   ½ cup (120 ml) cold water

1. Cut the peels off of the lemons and slice them into wedges. Core the apple and cut it into slices.

2. Juice the lemons, apple, and pineapple together, alternating the different kinds of produce as you juice (see page 23).

3. Mix the juice with the water. Serve immediately, over ice if desired.

◎ JUICY TIP

The essential oils contained in lemons contain 22 anticancer compounds. They also boost the immune system to help your body fight off infections and eliminate parasites.

Jalapeño Lemonade

Makes 12 to 16 ounces (355 to 475 ml)

Calling all juice lovers who love a little heat! Jalapeños add a kick without being too powerful. If you're tempted to try this but are a little leery, only use half of the jalapeño.

>   2 medium lemons
>   2 medium apples
>   1 jalapeño
>   1 cup (235 ml) cold water

1. Cut the peel off one of the lemons. Leave the peel on the other lemon. Slice the lemons into wedges. Core the apples and cut them into slices.

2. Juice the lemons, apples, and jalapeño together, alternating the different kinds of produce as you juice (see page 23).

3. Mix the juice with the water. Serve immediately, over ice if desired.

🌶 JUICY TIP

Jalapeños are great for blood circulation. Test them out in juices by only adding half of one to your first batch. If you can take the heat, add more the next time.

Carrot Lemonade

Makes 12 to 16 ounces (355 to 475 ml)

This beautiful orange-hued juice is a great way to up the nutritional benefits of traditional sweet lemonade.

2 medium lemons
2 medium apples
1 large carrot
½ cup (120 ml) cold water

1. Cut the peels off of the lemons and slice them into wedges. Core the apples and cut them into slices.

2. Juice the lemons, apples, and carrot together.

3. Mix the juice with the water. Serve immediately, over ice if desired.

Lime Mint Lemonade

Makes 12 to 16 ounces (355 to 475 ml)

This is one of the most refreshing lemonades you'll ever make. It's perfect for hydrating on a hot day.

2 medium apples
1 medium lemon
1 large lime
7 sprigs of fresh mint
½ cup (120 ml) cold water

1. Core the apples and cut them into slices. Cut the peel off of the lemon. Leave the peel on the lime. Slice the lemon and lime into wedges.

2. Juice the apples, lemon, lime, and mint together, alternating the different kinds of produce as you juice (see page 23).

3. Mix the juice with the water. Serve immediately, over ice if desired.

CHIA
JUICES

Chia is a seed of Peruvian origin that is high in omega-3s, antioxidants, protein, and fiber. Many people add chia seeds to baked goods, puddings, salads, and smoothies. One of the best ways to consume them is in fresh juice. Chia becomes gelatinous in liquid and so combines perfectly with juice, adding a nice texture and dense nutrients. These chia juices are like a healthful version of bubble tea without all the refined sugar and tapioca pearls.

Watermelon, Lime, and Chia Juice

Makes 12 to 16 ounces (355 to 475 ml)

This summertime juice is especially beautiful when made with white chia seeds.

> 1 lime
> 3 cups (450 g) watermelon chunks
> 1 tablespoon (13 g) chia seeds

1. Cut the peel off of the lime and cut it in half.

2. Juice the lime and watermelon together.

3. Stir in the chia seeds and allow them to soften for 5 minutes. Stir again and serve immediately.

☞ **JUICY TIP**
There are generally two types of chia seeds available in the market: white and black. They both have similar nutrients and texture.

Grape, Lemon, and Chia Juice ▶

Makes 12 to 16 ounces (355 to 475 ml)

I love this blend to curb sweet cravings. The lemon is so energizing!

> 1 lemon
> 3 cups (450 g) red grapes
> 2 celery stalks
> 1 tablespoon (13 g) chia seeds

1. Cut the peel off of the lemon and cut it in half.

2. Juice the lemon, grapes, and celery together.

3. Stir in the chia seeds and allow them to soften for 5 minutes. Stir again and serve immediately.

Mango, Strawberry, and Chia Juice

Makes 12 to 16 ounces (355 to 475 ml)

This is a thick and filling juice, wonderful as a meal replacement. You can use plain water instead of coconut water, if you like.

> 2 mangoes
> 20 strawberries
> 1 cup (235 ml) coconut water
> 1 tablespoon (13 g) chia seeds

1. Cut the peels off of the mangoes and discard the pits. Cut the flesh into spears or chunks.

2. Juice the mangoes and strawberries together, alternating the two kinds of produce as you juice (see page 23).

3. Add the coconut water to the juice and stir.

4. Stir in the chia seeds and allow them to soften for 5 minutes. Stir again and serve immediately.

Cranberry, Apple, Grape, and Chia Juice

Makes 12 to 16 ounces (355 to 475 ml)

Classic cran-apple-grape is made into a delightful chia juice. This one is perfect for the kids.

> 1 apple
> 2 cups (300 g) grapes
> ½ cup (50 g) cranberries
> 1 tablespoon (13 g) chia seeds

1. Core the apple and cut it into slices.

2. Juice the apple, grapes, and cranberries together, alternating the different kinds of produce as you juice (see page 23).

3. Stir in the chia seeds and allow them to soften for 5 minutes. Stir again and serve immediately.

☉ JUICY TIP

I find that chia juices taste best in fruit-only combinations, but feel free to make it green by mixing in a cup (55 g) or so of light leafy greens to any of the recipes in this chapter.

Pineapple, Coconut, and Chia Juice

Makes 12 to 16 ounces (355 to 475 ml)

If you feel like going tropical today, this should be your drink of choice.

2 cups (330 g) fresh pineapple chunks
1 cup (67 g) kale leaves
½ cup (120 ml) coconut water
1 tablespoon (13 g) chia seeds

1. Juice the pineapple and kale together, alternating the two kinds of produce as you juice (see page 23).

2. Add the coconut water to the juice and stir.

3. Stir in the chia seeds and allow them to soften for 5 minutes. Stir again and serve immediately.

Cucumber, Kale, and Chia Juice

Makes 12 to 16 ounces (355 to 475 ml)

Amazingly refreshing and delightfully sweet, this one is a keeper.

1 large cucumber
2 apples
2 kale leaves
1 tablespoon (13 g) chia seeds

1. Cut the cucumber into spears. Core the apples and cut them into slices.

2. Juice the cucumber, apples, and kale together, alternating the different kinds of produce as you juice (see page 23).

3. Stir in the chia seeds and allow them to soften for 5 minutes. Stir again and serve immediately.

☞ JUICY TIP
Chia seeds were revered by both the Mayans and the Aztecs for their amazing energizing and natural healing powers.

Apple, Orange, and Chia Juice

Makes 12 to 16 ounces (355 to 475 ml)

You'll feel like you're drinking liquid sunshine as you down this juice.

> 3 apples
> 2 oranges
> 1 tablespoon (13 g) chia seeds

1. Core the apples and cut them into slices. Cut the peels off of the oranges and slice them into wedges.

2. Juice the apples and oranges together.

3. Stir in the chia seeds and allow them to soften for 5 minutes. Stir again and serve immediately.

Carrot, Pineapple, and Chia Juice

Makes 12 to 16 ounces (355 to 475 ml)

This luscious chia combination is highly nourishing and completely satisfying.

> 5 carrots
> 3 cups (495 g) fresh pineapple chunks
> 1 tablespoon (13 g) chia seeds

1. Juice the carrots and pineapple together.

2. Stir in the chia seeds and allow them to soften for 5 minutes. Stir again and serve immediately.

◀ Strawberry, Lime, and Chia Juice

Makes 12 to 16 ounces (355 to 475 ml)

This amazing blend combines coconut water with fruit and chia seeds for a truly hydrating combination. You can also use plain water, if you like.

1 lime
10 strawberries
1 cup (235 ml) coconut water
1 tablespoon (13 g) chia seeds

1. Cut the peel off of the lime and cut it in half.

2. Juice the lime and strawberries together.

3. Add the coconut water to the juice and stir.

4. Stir in the chia seeds and allow them to soften for 5 minutes. Stir again and serve immediately.

◄ Peach, Cucumber, and Chia Juice

Makes 12 to 16 ounces (355 to 475 ml)

This is the perfect way to cool and hydrate after a hot yoga session.

> 3 peaches
> 1 large cucumber
> 1 tablespoon (13 g) chia seeds

1. Pit the peaches and cut them into slices. Cut the cucumber into spears.

2. Juice the peaches and cucumber together.

3. Stir in the chia seeds and allow them to soften for 5 minutes. Stir again and serve immediately.

Grapefruit, Beet, Apple, and Chia Juice

Makes 12 to 16 ounces (355 to 475 ml)

Highly cleansing and reviving, this chia combination doesn't disappoint.

> 2 grapefruits
> 1 apple
> ½ of a beet
> 1 tablespoon (13 g) chia seeds

1. Cut the peels off of the grapefruits and slice them into wedges. Core the apple and cut it into slices. Cut the piece of beet in half.

2. Juice the grapefruits, apple, and beet together.

3. Stir in the chia seeds and allow them to soften for 5 minutes. Stir again and serve immediately.

Carrot, Orange, and Chia Juice

Makes 12 to 16 ounces (355 to 475 ml)

This immune-boosting classic is one of my favorite chia juices.

> 2 oranges
> 6 carrots
> 1-inch (2.5 cm) piece fresh turmeric
> ½ cup (120 ml) cold water
> 1 tablespoon (13 g) chia seeds

1. Cut the peels off of the oranges and slice them into wedges.

2. Juice the oranges, carrots, and turmeric together.

3. Stir the water into the juice.

4. Stir in the chia seeds and allow them to soften for 5 minutes. Stir again and serve immediately.

Blueberry, Grape, and Chia Juice ▶

Makes 12 to 16 ounces (355 to 475 ml)

Turn back the clock with this antioxidant-packed juice.

> 2 cup (300 g) grapes
> 2 cups (290 g) blueberries
> ½ cup (120 ml) coconut water
> 1 tablespoon (13 g) chia seeds

1. Juice the grapes and blueberries together, alternating the two kinds of produce as you juice (see page 23).

2. Stir the coconut water into the juice.

3. Stir in the chia seeds and allow them to soften for 5 minutes. Stir again and serve immediately.

◀ Carrot, Apricot, and Chia Juice

Makes 12 to 16 ounces (355 to 475 ml)

Carrots enhance the silicon-rich apricots in this blend to encourage healthy skin, hair, and nails.

2 large apples
2 apricots
4 carrots
½ cup (120 ml) cold water
1 tablespoon (13 g) chia seeds

1. Core the apples and cut them into slices. Pit the apricots and cut them into slices.

2. Juice the apples, apricots, and carrots together.

3. Add the water to the juice.

4. Stir in the chia seeds and allow them to soften for 5 minutes. Stir again and serve immediately.

Blackberry, Pear, and Chia Juice

Makes 12 to 16 ounces (355 to 475 ml)

Allow yourself to indulge in blackberry bliss! Brace yourself for a thick, sweet treat.

3 pears
1 cup (145 g) blackberries
½ cup (120 ml) cold water
1 tablespoon (13 g) chia seeds

1. Core the pears and cut them into slices.

2. Juice the pears and blackberries together, alternating the two kinds of produce as you juice (see page 23).

3. Stir the water into the juice.

4. Stir in the chia seeds and allow them to soften for 5 minutes. Stir again and serve immediately.

☞ JUICY TIP
If you prefer to make a chia gel instead of waiting for the chia to soften in your juice, just mix 1 tablespoon (13 g) of chia seeds into 5 ounces (150 ml) of water and let the mixture sit for 5 to 10 minutes while you juice your produce. When you're done, mix some of the gel with your juice and serve immediately.

Raspberry, Apple, and Chia Juice

Makes 12 to 16 ounces (355 to 475 ml)

Apples sweeten up the antioxidant-rich raspberries in this beautiful blend.

2 large apples
1 small cucumber
1 cup (125 g) raspberries
1 tablespoon (13 g) chia seeds

1. Core the apples and cut them into slices. Cut the cucumber into spears.

2. Juice the apples, cucumber, and raspberries together, alternating the different kinds of produce as you juice (see page 23).

3. Stir in the chia seeds and allow them to soften for 5 minutes. Stir again and serve immediately.

☞ JUICY TIP

It is believed that chia seeds were consumed as early as 3000 BCE. They come from the desert plant *Salvia hispanica*, a member of the mint family that grows in the Americas. Over the centuries, chia seeds have been eaten as a grain, ground into flour, mixed into medicines, mixed with water, and pressed for omega-3 oil.

Apple, Mint, and Chia Juice

Makes 12 to 16 ounces (355 to 475 ml)

Do you need an energizing chia juice? This tangy blend will have you singing from the rooftops.

3 apples
1 lemon
2 sprigs of fresh mint
½ cup (120 ml) cold water
1 tablespoon (13 g) chia seeds

1. Core the apples and cut them into slices. Cut the peel off of the lemon and cut it in half.

2. Juice the apples, lemon, and mint together, alternating the different kinds of produce as you juice (see page 23).

3. Stir the water into the juice.

4. Stir in the chia seeds and allow them to soften for 5 minutes. Stir again and serve immediately.

◁ Mango, Pineapple, and Chia Juice

Makes 12 to 16 ounces (355 to 475 ml)

This candy-like but thirst-quenching blend is perfect for a midday reviver.

> 1 mango
> 3 cups (495 g) fresh pineapple chunks
> 1 tablespoon (13 g) chia seeds

1. Cut the peel off of the mango and discard the pit. Cut the flesh into spears or chunks.

2. Juice the mango and pineapple together.

3. Stir in the chia seeds and allow them to soften for 5 minutes. Stir again and serve immediately.

Orange, Beet, and Chia Juice

Makes 12 to 16 ounces (355 to 475 ml)

You'll think two things when you make this juice: First, it has a stunning color. Second, its flavor is amazing.

> 3 large oranges
> 1 beet
> 1 tablespoon (13 g) chia seeds

1. Cut the peels off of the oranges and slice them into wedges. Cut the beet into quarters.

2. Juice the oranges and beet together.

3. Stir in the chia seeds and allow them to soften for 5 minutes. Stir again and serve immediately.

☞ **JUICY TIP**
Chia seeds might help regulate blood sugar and contribute to weight loss. The gelling action of the seed and its unique combination of soluble and insoluble fibers combine to slow down your body's conversion of starches into sugars. Because the gel is made of water, it has no calories, and it helps your body to think it is full.

Green Pineapple Chia Juice

Makes 12 to 16 ounces (355 to 475 ml)

Sneak your greens into a chia juice with this delightful blend.

> 1 lime
> 3 cups (495 g) fresh pineapple chunks
> 2 romaine lettuce leaves
> 1 tablespoon (13 g) chia seeds

1. Cut the peel off of the lime and cut it in half.

2. Juice the lime, pineapple, and romaine lettuce together, alternating the different kinds of produce as you juice (see page 23).

3. Stir in the chia seeds and allow them to soften for 5 minutes. Stir again and serve immediately.

NUT MILK JUICES

If you're into silky, creamy drinks, then nut milk juices are for you. You might be surprised to know that mixing nut milks with your juices is a fabulous way to increase daily nutrition and switch up your juicing routine. You can use any type of nut milk and experiment with flavors. What's the best part? These blends are dairy-free and are loaded with healthful nutrients that will keep you full between meals.

How to Make Nut Milks

In order to make your own nut milk juices, you'll need to know how to make fresh nut milks. You could use the store-bought versions, but I don't recommend it. Prepackaged nut milks generally do not taste as good as homemade ones, and many of them have unhealthy additives you want to avoid. It's easy to make your own.

Simple, Basic Nut Milk

Makes about 3½ cups (825 ml)

You can use almost any type of fresh nuts for your nut milks. Make sure they are not roasted or salted. You'll want to use only fresh, raw nuts. The best nut milks, I think, are made from pecans, almonds, cashews, pistachios, walnuts, macadamias, or hazelnuts. If you are new to nut milk, start with cashew and almond milks.

- 1 cup (145 g) raw unroasted nuts (any variety)
- 3 cups (700 ml) filtered water
- 1 tablespoon (15 ml) pure vanilla extract
- 2 tablespoons (40 g) honey or pure maple syrup, or 2 pitted dates (optional, for a sweeter milk)
- 1 tablespoon (14 g) coconut butter (optional, for a thicker, creamier milk)

1. Soak the nuts in water to cover for at least 4 hours or up to overnight. Once the nuts are hydrated and plump, drain the nuts and discard the water.

2. Place the nuts, filtered water, and vanilla in a blender. Add the honey, syrup, or dates, if you like. For a creamier nut milk, also add the coconut butter. Blend on high speed until smooth. (A high-speed blender, such as a Vitamix or Blendtec, works the best to make silky smooth nut milks.) Once the milk is well combined, it's ready to be used. Store it in a glass container in the refrigerator.

☞ JUICY TIP

Many people like their nut milks unstrained. However, this often produces a thick milk that some people find undesirable. For a smooth milk with no nut sediment in it, strain it through a nut milk bag or a doubled layer of cheesecloth before consuming. The nut pulp can be used in cookies and other sweets.

Carrot Almond Milk Juice

Makes 12 to 16 ounces (355 to 475 ml)

This classic nut milk juice is creamy, sweet, and delightfully satisfying. You'll really appreciate its flavor.

> 5 carrots
> 1 cup (235 ml) almond milk (see
>   Simple, Basic Nut Milk, page 194)

1. Juice the carrots.

2. Pour the juice into a large glass and add the almond milk. Stir to combine. Serve immediately.

☞ **JUICY TIP**
Nut milk juices store well in the refrigerator, but only for about half a day. Store them in a glass jar with a tight-fitting lid and consume within 12 hours.

Blueberry Almond Milk Juice

Makes 12 to 16 ounces (355 to 475 ml)

Blueberry milk is a staple in my home. The blueberry flavor really stands out when you use almond milk.

> 1 cup (145 g) blueberries
> 1 cup (235 ml) almond milk (see
>   Simple, Basic Nut Milk, page 194)

1. Juice the blueberries.

2. Pour the juice into a large glass and add the almond milk. Stir to combine. Serve immediately.

◀ Peach Pecan Milk Juice

Makes 12 to 16 ounces (355 to 475 ml)

Peaches and pecans go well in a pie, so why not in a juice? This heavenly combination will satisfy your sweet tooth.

> 3 peaches
> 1 cup (235 ml) pecan milk (see Simple, Basic Nut Milk, page 194)

1. Pit the peaches and cut them into slices.

2. Juice the peaches.

3. Pour the juice into a large glass and add the pecan milk. Stir to combine. Serve immediately.

Mixed-Berry Pistachio Milk Juice

Makes 12 to 16 ounces (355 to 475 ml)

This milk reminds me of berry ice cream. Sweet and creamy, it doesn't get better than this!

> 1 cup (125 g) raspberries
> 1 cup (145 g) blueberries
> 1 cup (235 ml) pistachio milk (see Simple, Basic Nut Milk, page 194)

1. Juice the raspberries and blueberries together.

2. Pour the juice into a large glass and add the pistachio milk. Stir to combine. Serve immediately.

☞ **JUICY TIP**
Nut milk juices make great midday snacks because they almost always are more filling than regular juices.

Pineapple Cashew Milk Juice

Makes 12 to 16 ounces (355 to 475 ml)

This one tastes a little like a tropical yogurt. For a summertime treat, chill it in the refrigerator before consuming it.

> 1 cup (165 g) fresh pineapple chunks
> 1 cup (235 ml) cashew milk (see Simple, Basic Nut Milk, page 194)

1. Juice the pineapple.

2. Pour the juice into a large glass and add the cashew milk. Stir to combine. Serve immediately.

Mango Hazelnut Milk Juice

Makes 12 to 16 ounces (355 to 475 ml)

The light flavor of mango juice makes this hazelnut milk just perfect.

> 2 mangoes
> 1 cup (235 ml) hazelnut milk (see Simple, Basic Nut Milk, page 194)

1. Cut the peel off of the mangoes and discard the pits. Cut the flesh into spears or chunks.

2. Juice the mangoes.

3. Pour the juice into a large glass and add the hazelnut milk. Stir to combine. Serve immediately.

Raspberry Almond Milk Juice

Makes 12 to 16 ounces (355 to 475 ml)

The rose-hued color of this nut milk is gorgeous, and the juice tastes amazing. Raspberries yield a thick juice that blends nicely with nut milk.

> 1 cup (125 g) raspberries
> 1 cup (235 ml) almond milk (see Simple, Basic Nut Milk, page 194)

1. Juice the raspberries.

2. Pour the juice into a large glass and add the almond milk. Stir to combine. Serve immediately.

☞ **JUICY TIP**
To make the silkiest nut milks, use a high-powered, high-speed blender. These blenders have the ability to chop through the nuts effortlessly to make a smooth and creamy milk.

Cherry Pistachio Milk Juice

Makes 12 to 16 ounces (355 to 475 ml)

This stunning milk is a great summertime treat and one that helps reduce uric acid in the body.

1½ cups (233 g) cherries
1 cup (235 ml) pistachio milk (see Simple, Basic Nut Milk, page 194)

1. Pit the cherries.

2. Juice the cherries.

3. Pour the juice into a large glass and add the pistachio milk. Stir to combine. Serve immediately.

Peach Cinnamon Cashew Milk Juice

Makes 12 to 16 ounces (355 to 475 ml)

Do you have some Georgia peaches lying around? This crowd-pleaser tastes like dessert and is perfect for serving as one.

3 peaches
1 cup (235 ml) cashew milk (see Simple, Basic Nut Milk, page 194)
¼ teaspoon ground cinnamon

1. Pit the peaches and cut them into slices.

2. Juice the peaches.

3. Pour the juice into a large glass. Add the cashew milk and cinnamon. Stir to combine. Serve immediately.

Strawberry Hazelnut Milk Juice

Makes 12 to 16 ounces (355 to 475 ml)

If strawberries are your favorite, you must try this silky and fruity nut milk juice. You might want to add some maple syrup or honey to make it a bit sweeter.

> 10 strawberries
> 1 cup (235 ml) hazelnut milk (see
>   Simple, Basic Nut Milk, page 194)

1. Juice the strawberries.

2. Pour the juice into a large glass and add the hazelnut milk. Stir to combine. Serve immediately.

Strawberry Mango Cashew Milk Juice

Makes 12 to 16 ounces (355 to 475 ml)

This fruity combination makes a sunny start to any day.

> 1 mango
> 8 strawberries
> 1 cup (235 ml) cashew milk (see
>   Simple, Basic Nut Milk, page 194)

1. Cut the peel off of the mango and discard the pit. Cut the flesh into spears or chunks.

2. Juice the mango and strawberries together.

3. Pour the juice into a large glass and add the cashew milk. Stir to combine. Serve immediately.

◄ Strawberry Almond Milk Juice

Makes 12 to 16 ounces (355 to 475 ml)

Everyone loves strawberry milk. This nondairy version isn't the powdery sweet kind. It's better. Feel free to blend in some pitted dates if you'd like your juice sweeter.

10 strawberries
1 cup (235 ml) almond milk (see
Simple, Basic Nut Milk, page 194)

1. Juice the strawberries.

2. Pour the juice into a large glass and add the almond milk. Stir to combine. Serve immediately.

Apricot Almond Milk Juice ▶

Makes 12 to 16 ounces (355 to 475 ml)

Almonds are highly nutritious and are loaded with vitamins to support brain development and promote healthy hair and nails. When you combine them with apricots, you've got yourself a nutrient-rich drink.

> **5 apricots**
> **1 cup (235 ml) almond milk (see Simple, Basic Nut Milk, page 194)**

1. Pit the apricots and cut them into slices.

2. Juice the apricots.

2. Pour the juice into a large glass and add the almond milk. Stir to combine. Serve immediately.

Chocolate Strawberry Cashew Milk Juice

Makes 12 to 16 ounces (355 to 475 ml)

Everyone knows chocolate-dipped strawberries taste fabulous. Try them in a nut milk version.

10 strawberries
1 cup (235 ml) cashew milk (see Simple, Basic Nut Milk, page 194)
1 tablespoon (5 g) unsweetened cocoa powder
1 tablespoon (20 g) honey (optional, for extra sweetness)

1. Juice the strawberries.

2. Pour the juice into a large glass. Add the cashew milk, cocoa powder, and, if you like, the honey. Stir to combine. Serve immediately.

Peach Pistachio Milk Juice

Makes 12 to 16 ounces (355 to 475 ml)

Peaches and pistachios are a pair made in heaven. The sweet-and-savory flavor profile is out of this world.

3 peaches
1 cup (235 ml) pistachio milk (see Simple, Basic Nut Milk, page 194)

1. Pit the peaches and cut them into slices.

2. Juice the peaches.

3. Pour the juice into a large glass and add the pistachio milk. Stir to combine. Serve immediately.

☞ **JUICY TIP**
Make sure you use only unroasted and unsalted nuts to make your nut milks. Roasted nuts result in an undesirable flavor and are not as nutritious as raw nuts.

Blueberry Macadamia Milk Juice

Makes 12 to 16 ounces (355 to 475 ml)

Macadamia nuts are pricey but make wonderful nut milks. Your kids might love this particular combination.

1 cup (145 g) blueberries
1 cup (235 ml) macadamia milk (see Simple, Basic Nut Milk, page 194)

1. Juice the blueberries.

2. Pour the juice into a large glass and add the macadamia milk. Stir to combine. Serve immediately.

Blackberry Vanilla Cashew Milk Juice ▶

Makes 12 to 16 ounces (355 to 475 ml)

Vanilla adds a nice complement to the blackberries in this creamy milk.

1 cup (145 g) blackberries
1 cup (235 ml) cashew milk (see Simple, Basic Nut Milk, page 194)
1 teaspoon pure vanilla extract

1. Juice the blackberries.

2. Pour the juice into a large glass. Add the cashew milk and vanilla. Stir to combine. Serve immediately.

☞ **JUICY TIP**
Don't be afraid to experiment with natural extracts to flavor nut milks. Extracts of any variety can pair well in many combinations. Lemon, vanilla, mint, and orange extracts are all good options.

◄ Carrot Cashew Milk Juice

Makes 12 to 16 ounces (355 to 475 ml)

Carrots and cashews are a perfect pair. If you don't like straight carrot juice, you might like this mellower option instead.

    5 carrots
    1 cup (235 ml) cashew milk (see
        Simple, Basic Nut Milk, page 194)

1. Juice the carrots.

2. Pour the juice into a large glass and add the cashew milk. Stir to combine. Serve immediately.

> 🥣 **JUICY TIP**
> Add 1 tablespoon (14 g) of coconut butter to any nut milk juice to boost nutrients and create a silky, creamy flavor.

Sweet Potato Pear Hazelnut Milk Juice

Makes 12 to 16 ounces (355 to 475 ml)

This recipe produces a filling juice that is perfect for a meal replacement or for midmorning nourishment.

    1 pear
    ½ of a medium sweet potato
    ½ cup (120 ml) hazelnut milk (see
        Simple, Basic Nut Milk, page 194)

1. Core the pear and cut it into slices. Cut the sweet potato into spears.

2. Juice the sweet potato and pear together.

3. Pour the juice into a large glass and add the hazelnut milk. Stir to combine. Serve immediately.

Pineapple Apricot Pecan Milk Juice

Makes 12 to 16 ounces (355 to 475 ml)

This unusual combination is sure to be a winner in your home.

> 1 apricot
> 1 cup (165 g) fresh pineapple chunks
> 1 cup (235 ml) pecan milk (see Simple, Basic Nut Milk, page 194)

1. Pit the apricot and cut it into slices.

2. Juice the apricot and pineapple together.

3. Pour the juice into a large glass and add the pecan milk. Stir to combine. Serve immediately.

☞ **JUICY TIP**
Many higher-end slow juicers can make nut milk juice easier to prepare. Typically, you'll soak the nuts in filtered water overnight and then juice them right along with the fruit or vegetable. Check your juicer's manual to see if your model has this feature.

Pear Walnut Milk Juice

Makes 12 to 16 ounces (355 to 475 ml)

The crisp pears lighten up the richer walnut taste. It's delightful.

> 2 pears
> 1 cup (235 ml) walnut milk (see Simple, Basic Nut Milk, page 194)

1. Core the pears and cut them into slices.

2. Juice the pears.

3. Pour the juice into a large glass and add the walnut milk. Stir to combine. Serve immediately.

Turmeric Macadamia Milk Juice

Makes 12 to 16 ounces (355 to 475 ml)

Turmeric is an amazing root, often used to combat inflammation. Surprisingly, it tastes delicious in this nut milk, which is extremely healthful to drink daily. Feel free to add your favorite fruit to this recipe for a tasty twist.

4-inch (10 cm) piece of fresh turmeric
1½ (355 ml) cups macadamia milk (see Simple, Basic Nut Milk, page 194)
1 tablespoon (14 g) coconut butter

1. Juice the turmeric. You won't get much juice, but it is potent.

2. Pour the turmeric juice and the macadamia milk into a large glass. Add the coconut butter. Stir to combine. Serve immediately.

Carrot Mango Cashew Milk Juice

Makes 12 to 16 ounces (355 to 475 ml)

Carrots pair so beautifully with mango and cashews in this silky milk. It's one of my all-time favorites.

1 mango
3 large carrots
1 cup (235 ml) cashew milk (see Simple, Basic Nut Milk, page 194)

1. Cut the peel off of the mango and discard the pit. Cut the flesh into spears or chunks.

2. Juice the carrots and mango together.

3. Pour the juice into a large glass and add the cashew milk. Stir to combine. Serve immediately.

Gingered Peachy Pear Walnut Milk Juice

Makes 12 to 16 ounces (355 to 475 ml)

This spicy milk juice tastes like peach pie. Who wouldn't love that?

  1 peach
  1 pear
  1-inch (2.5 cm) piece of fresh ginger
  1 cup (235 ml) walnut milk (see
    Simple, Basic Nut Milk, page 194)

1. Pit the peach and cut it into slices. Core the pear and cut it into slices.

2. Juice the peach, pear, and ginger together.

3. Pour the juice into a large glass and add the walnut milk. Stir to combine. Serve immediately.

Apple Cinnamon Pecan Milk Juice ▶

Makes 12 to 16 ounces (355 to 475 ml)

Do you feel like having a piece of apple pie without the calories? Try this milk instead.

  1 apple
  1 cup (235 ml) pecan milk (see
    Simple, Basic Nut Milk, page 194)
  ½ teaspoon ground cinnamon

1. Core the apple and cut it into slices.

2. Juice the apple.

3. Pour the juice into a large glass and add the pecan milk and cinnamon. Stir to combine. Serve immediately.

☞ **JUICY TIP**
If you favor sweeter nut milk, there are a few healthful additions you can incorporate. Add a few drops of stevia or 1 tablespoon (20 g) of honey or blend 1 pitted date into the milk.

KID-FRIENDLY
JUICES

I can't think of a better way to supercharge a child's diet than by serving nutrient-rich fresh juices. Ditch the artificially colored and heavily sugared juices from the supermarket and opt for the real thing in these taste-tested, kid-approved blends.

Red Rainbow Juice

Makes 12 to 16 ounces (355 to 475 ml)

This juice is bursting with color and flavor that everyone in the family will love.

> 1 beet
> 1 apple
> 2 cups (300 g) watermelon chunks
> 1 cup (125 g) raspberries

1. Cut the beet into quarters. Core the apple and cut it into slices.

2. Juice the beet, apple, watermelon, and raspberries together, alternating the different kinds of produce as you juice (see page 23). Serve immediately.

ABC Juice

Makes 12 to 16 ounces (355 to 475 ml)

This rich red juice is full of nutrients for a growing body.

> 2 apples
> 1 beet
> 4 celery stalks
> ½ cup (120 ml) coconut water

1. Core the apples and cut them into slices. Cut the beet into quarters.

2. Juice the apples, beet, and celery together. Add the coconut water and stir to combine. Serve immediately.

🥣 JUICY TIP
Feel free to dilute any of your juices with 1 cup (235 ml) of water or coconut water to lighten the flavor. You can do this for your own juices, and it works especially well for children who prefer a milder juice.

◀ Super Celery Cooler

Makes 12 to 16 ounces (355 to 475 ml)

This sweet hydrator is perfect served over ice on a hot summer day.

> 2 apples
> 1 kiwifruit
> 4 celery stalks

1. Core the apples and cut them into slices. Peel the kiwi and cut it in half.

2. Juice the apples, kiwi, and celery together. Serve immediately.

Popeye Punch

Makes 12 to 16 ounces (355 to 475 ml)

Popeye got strong by eating lots of spinach, and so can your kids!

> 1 apple
> 1 pear
> 1 cup (165 g) fresh pineapple chunks
> 2 cups (60 g) spinach leaves

1. Core the apple and pear and cut them into slices.

2. Juice the apple, pear, pineapple, and spinach together, alternating the different kinds of produce as you juice (see page 23). Serve immediately.

Radical Radish

Makes 12 to 16 ounces (355 to 475 ml)

Does your child have sinus issues? This gentle radish juice might help his or her sinuses clear up naturally.

>   2 apples
>   5 carrots
>   1 radish

1. Core the apples and cut them into slices.

2. Juice the apples, carrots, and radish together. Serve immediately.

All-Star Favorite ▶

Makes 12 to 16 ounces (355 to 475 ml)

This classic blend is always a taste-test winner among kids.

>   3 oranges
>   5 carrots

1. Cut the peels off of the oranges and slice them into wedges.

2. Juice the oranges and carrots together. Serve immediately.

Magical Melon

Makes 12 to 16 ounces (355 to 475 ml)

This pink-hued melon juice is delightfully hydrating and extremely flavorful.

> 3 cups (480 g) cantaloupe chunks
> 1 cup (165 g) fresh pineapple chunks
> 5 strawberries

1. Juice the cantaloupe, pineapple, and strawberries together, alternating the different kinds of produce as you juice (see page 23). Serve immediately.

Awesome Apple

Makes 12 to 16 ounces (355 to 475 ml)

Every kid loves the classic apple juice. Spice it up with grapes and you'll have a winner every time.

> 4 red apples
> 2 cups (300 g) grapes

1. Core the apples and cut them into slices.

2. Juice the apples and grapes together. Serve immediately.

Green Power Punch

Makes 12 to 16 ounces (355 to 475 ml)

This juice successfully hides the calcium-rich broccoli, making it ideal for kids who think they don't like broccoli.

> 2 apples
> 1 pear
> ½ of a cucumber
> 2 broccoli florets

1. Core the apples and cut them into slices. Core the pear and cut it into slices. Cut the cucumber half into spears.

2. Juice the apples, pear, cucumber, and broccoli together. Serve immediately.

Dinosaur Power

Makes 12 to 16 ounces (355 to 475 ml)

Don't forget to tell your kids that the dinosaurs ate a ton of leafy greens. This drink is packed with them.

2 apples
1 cucumber
½ of a lime
1 bunch of spinach leaves
1 kale leaf

1. Core the apples and cut them into slices. Cut the cucumber into spears. Cut the peel off of the lime half.

2. Juice the apples, cucumber, lime, spinach, and kale together, alternating the different kinds of produce as you juice (see page 23). Serve immediately.

🥕 JUICY TIP
Strong juices, like those that contain spinach, watercress, kale, parsley, or beets, are good for children, but in smaller and gentler doses. You'll want to dilute these juices with milder and sweeter varieties of produce.

Radically Red Berry

Makes 12 to 16 ounces (355 to 475 ml)

Every kid loves this berry-licious drink!

2 apples
½ of a cucumber
10 strawberries
1 cup (125 g) raspberries

1. Core the apples and cut them into slices. Cut the cucumber half into spears.

2. Juice the apples, cucumber, strawberries, and raspberries together, alternating the different kinds of produce as you juice (see page 23). Serve immediately.

Joyful Jamberry

Makes 12 to 16 ounces (355 to 475 ml)

This berry version of orange juice is a great afternoon snack for children. Feel free to add some light leafy greens to this juice for additional nutrients.

4 oranges
10 strawberries

1. Cut the peels off of the oranges and slice them into wedges.

2. Juice the oranges and strawberries together, alternating the two kinds of produce as you juice (see page 23). Serve immediately.

Cheerful Cherry

Makes 12 to 16 ounces (355 to 475 ml)

Three cheers for this lively combination that includes vitamin C–rich cherries.

2 pears
½ of a cucumber
1 cup (155 g) cherries
2 cups (300 g) watermelon chunks

1. Core the pears and cut them it into slices. Cut the cucumber half into spears. Pit the cherries.

2. Juice the pears, cucumber, cherries, and watermelon together, alternating the different kinds of produce as you juice (see page 23). Serve immediately.

Lovely Lemon

Makes 12 to 16 ounces (355 to 475 ml)

This natural lemonade is sweetened with apples to balance the tartness. If your kids don't mind green juice, add a handful of romaine lettuce leaves to this blend.

4 apples
1 lemon

1. Core the apples and cut them into slices. Cut the peel off of the lemon and cut it in half.

2. Juice the apples and lemon together. Serve immediately.

◄ Wild Watermelon

Makes 12 to 16 ounces (355 to 475 ml)

Watermelon is perfect for outdoor picnics and hot days but can get messy when the kids eat it. So juice it instead.

3 cups (450 g) watermelon chunks
1 cup (125 g) raspberries
1 cup (235 ml) coconut water

1. Juice the watermelon and raspberries together, alternating the two kinds of produce as you juice (see page 23).

2. Stir in the coconut water. Serve immediately.

Green Monster

Makes 12 to 16 ounces (355 to 475 ml)

This juice is green in color but sweet in flavor. It's an incredibly easy way to get broccoli into a child's diet.

> 3 cups (495 g) fresh pineapple chunks
> 3 broccoli florets

1. Juice the pineapple and broccoli together. Serve immediately.

🥦 **JUICY TIP**

Hide nutritionally dense vegetables such as broccoli in juices with fruits. Your picky eaters will never detect them.

Wacky Strawberry

Makes 12 to 16 ounces (355 to 475 ml)

It's not often I meet a kid who doesn't like this juicy apple and strawberry blend.

> 2 apples
> 1 cucumber
> 15 strawberries

1. Core the apples and cut them into slices. Cut the cucumber into spears.

2. Juice the apples, cucumber, and strawberries together, alternating the different kinds of produce as you juice (see page 23). Serve immediately.

Bodacious Berry

Makes 12 to 16 ounces (355 to 475 ml)

This juice is the perfect thing to make after a day of strawberry picking.

> 2 apples
> 10 strawberries
> 1 cup (145 g) blueberries
> 4 celery stalks

1. Core the apples and cut them into slices.

2. Juice the apples, strawberries, blueberries, and celery together, alternating the different kinds of produce as you juice (see page 23). Serve immediately.

Crazy Cranberry Apple

Makes 12 to 16 ounces (355 to 475 ml)

Cranberries are full of nutrients, but most kids don't like them unless they are sweetened. The four apples in this recipe do the trick nicely. Note: Save some of this juice for yourself.

4 red apples
1 cup (100 g) cranberries
3 celery stalks

1. Core the apples and cut them into slices.

2. Juice the apples, cranberries, and celery together, alternating the different kinds of produce as you juice (see page 23). Serve immediately.

Bashful Blueberry

Makes 12 to 16 ounces (355 to 475 ml)

No one will be bashful after drinking this blueberry juice! It's sure to bring a smile to everyone's faces.

1 apple
1 medium cucumber
2 cups (290 g) blueberries

1. Core the apple and cut it into slices. Cut the cucumber into spears.

2. Juice the apple, cucumber, and blueberries together, alternating the different kinds of produce as you juice (see page 23). Serve immediately.

◀ Clever Cucumber

Makes 12 to 16 ounces (355 to 475 ml)

Cucumbers are a great way to hydrate. If you like, mix some sparkling water into this blend to make it a juice soda.

> 1 large cucumber
> 2 cups (300 g) green grapes

1. Cut the cucumber into spears.

2. Juice the cucumber and grapes together. Serve immediately.

Yummy Carrot Craze

Makes 12 to 16 ounces (355 to 475 ml)

Carrots are high in beta-carotene, which is critical for healthy development in kids.

> 1 pear
> ½ of a cucumber
> 6 carrots

1. Core the pear and cut it into slices. Cut the cucumber half into spears.

2. Juice the pear, cucumber, and carrots together. Serve immediately.

Mighty Mango

Makes 12 to 16 ounces (355 to 475 ml)

Mangoes are densely textured and sweet, and most kids love them mixed with orange juice.

> 3 oranges
> 1 mango
> ½ of a lime

1. Cut the peel off of the oranges and slice them into wedges. Cut the peel off of the mango and discard the pit. Cut the flesh into spears or chunks. Cut the peel off of the lime half.

2. Juice the oranges, mango, and lime together. Serve immediately.

Fantastic Pear Punch

Makes 12 to 16 ounces (355 to 475 ml)

This tasty punch will be asked for over and over again.

> 3 pears
> 6 celery stalks

1. Core the pears and cut them into slices.

2. Juice the pears and celery together. Serve immediately.

◀ Tangerine Tang

Makes 12 to 16 ounces (355 to 475 ml)

Kids think this natural take-off on the commercial powdered drink is amazing.

2 oranges
5 tangerines

1. Cut the peels off of the oranges and slice them into wedges. Cut the peels off of the tangerines.

2. Juice the oranges and tangerines together. Serve immediately.

☞ **JUICY TIP**
When juicing for your kids, start out with fruity blends and then slowly add in vegetables to other batches of juice to help them get used to the taste.

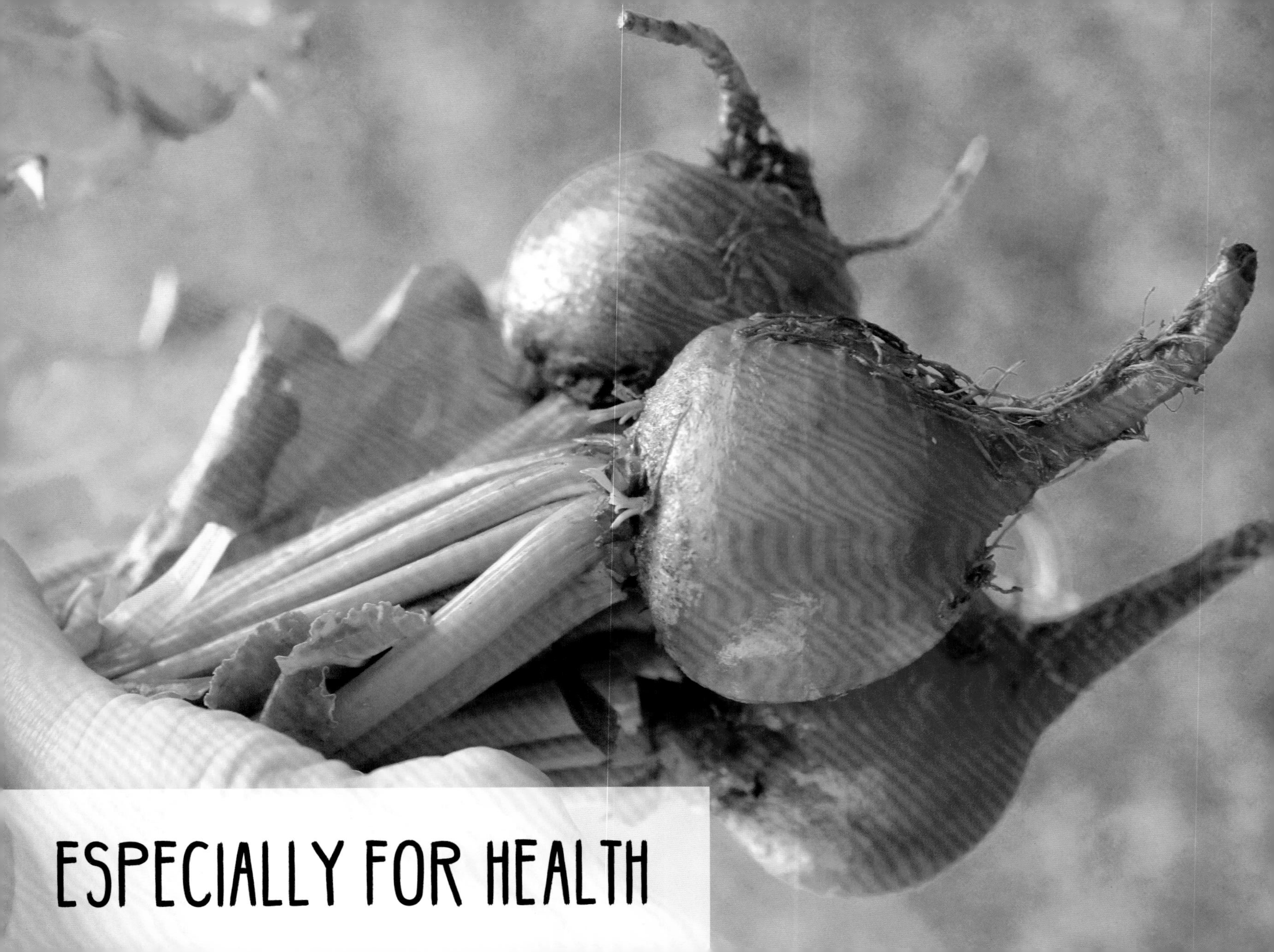

ESPECIALLY FOR HEALTH

ENERGY
JUICES

Sometimes we need a little jolt of energy in the morning or at midday to boost the brain and the body. The nutrition in fresh fruits and veggies assists your body so it can function in high-performance mode. These combinations will help you get the "juice high" you're looking for. Put down the coffee and reach for an energy-centered juice.

Green Jolt

Makes 12 to 16 ounces (355 to 475 ml)

This precious juice is like a lightning bolt of energy in your day.

> 2 apples
> 5 large carrots
> 1 handful of fresh parsley
> 1 broccoli stalk

1. Core the apples and cut them into slices.

2. Juice the apples, carrots, parsley, and broccoli together, alternating the different kinds of produce as you juice (see page 23). Serve immediately.

Triple Power

Makes 12 to 16 ounces (355 to 475 ml)

This ingredient trio makes a great morning energizer.

> 2 grapefruits
> 1 large apple
> 5 kale leaves

1. Cut the peels off of the grapefruits and slice them into wedges. Core the apple and cut it into slices.

2. Juice the grapefruits, apple, and kale together, alternating the different kinds of produce as you juice (see page 23). Serve immediately.

Pineapple Kick ▶

Makes 12 to 16 ounces (355 to 475 ml)

Wheatgrass is a great energizer that combines well with pineapple. Adding it to any juice will keep you going on raw natural energy for hours.

> ½ of a fresh pineapple
> 4 romaine lettuce leaves
> 1 handful of wheatgrass

1. Cut the pineapple half into spears.

2. Juice the pineapple, romaine lettuce, and wheatgrass together, alternating the different kinds of produce as you juice (see page 23). Serve immediately.

☞ **JUICY TIP**
Some juicers can juice wheatgrass and some can't. Typically, it's the single- or twin-gear juicers that can handle it. You can also purchase a separate manual wheatgrass juicer. If you don't have access to fresh wheatgrass, frozen cubes and wheatgrass powder are readily available in health food stores.

Wheatgrass Reviver

Makes 12 to 16 ounces (355 to 475 ml)

I'm a huge fan of wheatgrass—it has never let me down. Keep frozen pre-juiced wheatgrass ice cubes in your freezer to melt in your juice so that you don't have to keep fresh wheatgrass on hand all the time.

> 6 carrots
> 4 celery stalks
> 1 handful of wheatgrass

1. Juice the carrots, celery, and wheatgrass together, alternating the different kinds of produce as you juice (see page 23). (If you have one, juice the wheatgrass in a wheatgrass juicer or masticating juicer separately to get the maximum amount of liquid from the grass.) Serve immediately.

☞ **JUICY TIP**
Try to stick mostly to low-sugar, vegetable-based juices when you are juicing for energy. Too much sugar can suppress your immune system.

Orange Vitality

Makes 12 to 16 ounces (355 to 475 ml)

This orange and kale blend not only tastes great, but it's also full of energizing nutrients.

> 2 oranges
> 2 green apples
> 4 kale leaves

1. Cut the peel off of the oranges and slice them into wedges. Core the apples and cut them into slices.

2. Juice the oranges, apples, and kale together, alternating the different kinds of produce as you juice (see page 23). Serve immediately.

Red Zing

Makes 12 to 16 ounces (355 to 475 ml)

This combination of beet, carrots, and kale will stimulate your entire system.

> 1 red beet
> 6 large carrots
> 2 kale leaves

1. Cut the beet into quarters.

2. Juice the beet, carrots, and kale together, alternating the different kinds of produce as you juice (see page 23). Serve immediately.

Carrot Pep-Up

Makes 12 to 16 ounces (355 to 475 ml)

This very veggie combo is a great midday juice to keep you going strong.

> 1 red bell pepper
> 8 large carrots
> 1 small handful of fresh cilantro

1. Cut the stem off of the bell pepper and cut it into strips.

2. Juice the carrots, pepper, and cilantro together, alternating the different kinds of produce as you juice (see page 23). Serve immediately.

Parsley Power

Makes 12 to 16 ounces (355 to 475 ml)

Mixing chlorophyll-rich parsley and warming ginger together in this juice will invigorate your whole body by increasing your circulation and helping to oxidize your blood.

> 1 lemon
> 1 large cucumber
> 1 apple
> 1-inch (2.5 cm) piece of fresh ginger
> 1 handful of fresh parsley

1. Cut the peel off of the lemon and cut it into slices. Cut the cucumber into spears. Core the apple and cut it into slices.

2. Juice the lemon, cucumber, apple, ginger, and parsley together, alternating the different kinds of produce as you juice (see page 23). Serve immediately.

◀ Sweet Potato Buzz

Makes 12 to 16 ounces (355 to 475 ml)

This is a personal favorite when I need a pick-me-up. Bonus: This one's good for glowing skin.

> 3 sweet potatoes
> 4 large carrots
> 1 handful of fresh parsley

1. Cut the sweet potatoes into spears.

2. Juice the sweet potatoes, carrots, and parsley together, alternating the different kinds of produce as you juice (see page 23). Serve immediately.

☞ **JUICY TIP**
Adding parsley to any juice will boost its energy power. Parsley has properties to energize and cleanse your entire system. It is one of the highest sources of chlorophyll, which acts like iron to oxygenate the blood. People all over the world use parsley in their juices to enhance their energy before workouts.

Green Stimulant

Makes 12 to 16 ounces (355 to 475 ml)

This juice has everything you need to keep you in overdrive all day long. I like it as a pre-workout hydrator and energy booster.

> 1 apple
> 4 celery stalks
> 2 carrots
> 1 cucumber
> 1 large handful of watercress

1. Core the apple and cut it into slices.

2. Juice the apple, celery, carrots, cucumber, and watercress together, alternating the different kinds of produce as you juice (see page 23). Serve immediately.

Morning Magic

Makes 12 to 16 ounces (355 to 475 ml)

Are you thinking about replacing coffee with juice? This magical blend will do the trick.

 2 apples
 1 pear
 ½ of a cucumber
 3 romaine lettuce leaves
 2 kale leaves
 ½-inch (1.3 cm) piece of fresh ginger

1. Core the apples and cut them into slices. Core the pear and cut it into slices. Cut the cucumber half into spears.

2. Juice the apples, pear, cucumber, romaine lettuce, kale, and ginger together, alternating the different kinds of produce as you juice (see page 23). Serve immediately.

> ☞ **JUICY TIP**
> When creating your own energy juices, don't forget the greens. The chlorophyll and vitamins in leafy greens promote energy power in your body.

Electric Cocktail

Makes 12 to 16 ounces (355 to 475 ml)

This juice has amazing flavor, and it's one of those juices you can keep adding kale to without tasting it.

 1 sweet potato
 1 pear
 ½ of a cucumber
 2 cups (290 g) strawberries
 5 kale leaves

1. Cut the sweet potato into spears. Core the pear and cut it into slices. Cut the cucumber half into spears.

2. Juice the sweet potato, pear, cucumber, strawberries, and kale together, alternating the different kinds of produce as you juice (see page 23). Serve immediately.

◀ Green Fix

Makes 12 to 16 ounces (355 to 475 ml)

This amazing juice tastes like a green lemonade and really gives you a "juice high." You'll never detect the greens as you drink it.

> 1 medium cucumber
> 1 pear
> 1 lime
> 2 large romaine lettuce leaves
> 1 cup (30 g) spinach leaves

1. Cut the cucumber into spears. Core the pear and cut it into slices. Leave the peel on the lime and cut it in half.

2. Juice the cucumber, pear, lime, romaine lettuce, and spinach together, alternating the different kinds of produce as you juice (see page 23). Serve immediately.

◀ Lime Zing

Makes 12 to 16 ounces (355 to 475 ml)

Spirulina is a powerhouse of nutrients and will give you energy. It combines well in this juice, a great drink if you're on the go.

> 3 large apples
> 1 large lemon
> 1 large lime
> 1 teaspoon spirulina powder

1. Core the apples and cut them into slices. Cut the peel off of the lemon and cut it in half. Cut the peel off of the lime and cut it in half.

2. Juice the apples, lemon, and lime together. Stir in the spirulina powder. Serve immediately.

Energy Elixir

Makes 12 to 16 ounces (355 to 475 ml)

You can't beat the nutrition this juice gives you. It will make you feel fabulous!

> 2 apples
> 5 large carrots
> 2 cups (60 g) spinach leaves

1. Core the apples and cut them into slices.

2. Juice the apples, carrots, and spinach together, alternating the different kinds of produce as you juice (see page 23). Serve immediately.

☞ JUICY TIP
Try adding a few drops of an herbal tincture to boost energy. My favorites are Siberian ginseng and astragulus root, both of which support the adrenal system.

CALMING
JUICES

Whether you need to relax from a stressful situation or you have insomnia, juice can be your savior to help you regain peace naturally as well as to bridge any nutritional gaps. In these calming juices, I have combined produce and herbs that have been used medicinally for centuries. These tasty blends can be enjoyed on a daily basis to keep the calm in your life.

Stress-Free Cocktail

Makes 12 to 16 ounces (355 to 475 ml)

Foods that are rich in vitamin C may help regulate and prevent spikes in cortisol, a stress hormone.

>   2 large oranges
>   1 cup (145 g) blueberries
>   1 cup (145 g) strawberries

1. Cut the peels off of the oranges and slice them into wedges.

2. Juice the oranges, blueberries, and strawberries together, alternating the different kinds of produce as you juice (see page 23). Serve immediately.

Tension Tamer Tonic

Makes 12 to 16 ounces (355 to 475 ml)

Sage is a valuable calming aid for the nervous excitement that frequently accompanies brain and nervous diseases. Celery is a nervine that also can help calm tension.

>   1 pear
>   1 cucumber
>   5 celery stalks
>   1 handful of fresh sage leaves

1. Core the pear and cut it into slices. Cut the cucumber into spears.

2. Juice the pear, cucumber, celery, and sage together, alternating the different kinds of produce as you juice (see page 23). Serve immediately.

Bedtime Flip

Makes 12 to 16 ounces (355 to 475 ml)

Some studies have shown that kiwifruit may improve sleep quality. This low-sugar juice is perfect before bed. Add coconut water if you want a little additional sweetness.

> 3 kiwifruits
> 1 large cucumber
> 3 celery stalks

1. Peel the kiwis and cut them in half. Cut the cucumber into spears.

2. Juice the kiwis, cucumber, and celery together. Serve immediately.

Sleepy Punch ▶

Makes 12 to 16 ounces (355 to 475 ml)

Cherries and raspberries are often consumed to help combat insomnia and ease the way to quality sleep.

> 1 large cucumber
> 1 cup (155 g) cherries
> 1 apple
> ½ cup (125 g) raspberries

1. Cut the cucumber into spears. Pit the cherries. Core the apple and cut it into slices.

2. Juice the cucumber, cherries, apple, and raspberries together, alternating the different kinds of produce as you juice (see page 23). Serve immediately.

Relax-tini ▶

Makes 12 to 16 ounces (355 to 475 ml)

Essential oils and minerals in celery juice can help calm nerves and can act as a natural sleep aid.

> **4 apples**
> **½ of a lime**
> **6 celery stalks**

1. Core the apples and cut them into slices. Cut the peel off of the lime half.

2. Juice the apple, lime, and celery together. Serve immediately.

Midday Calmer

Makes 12 to 16 ounces (355 to 475 ml)

The magnesium in chard may help balance levels of cortisol, the body's stress hormone.

> **2 apples**
> **1 cucumber**
> **2 Swiss chard leaves**

1. Core the apples and cut them into slices. Cut the cucumber into spears.

2. Juice the apples, cucumber, and Swiss chard together, alternating the different kinds of produce as you juice (see page 23). Serve immediately.

Tranquil Toddy

Makes 12 to 16 ounces (355 to 475 ml)

Spinach is high in the amino acid tryptophan, which can help to elevate your mood and promote better sleep. It's also high in magnesium, which helps to relax nerves and muscles.

    5 carrots
    3 cups (90 g) spinach leaves
    2 cups (330 g) fresh pineapple chunks

1. Juice the carrots, spinach, and pineapple together, alternating the different kinds of produce as you juice (see page 23). Serve immediately.

☞ **JUICY TIP**
Try brewing a mild herbal tea, such as chamomile, and mixing some into your juice to enhance the calming nutrients.

Peaceful Breeze

Makes 12 to 16 ounces (355 to 475 ml)

Tarragon promotes calmness and is an herbal remedy that has been used for thousands of years for calming hyperactive children. It is a very good herb for stress relief.

    1 apple
    1 cucumber
    ½ of a lemon
    1 small handful of watercress
    1 small handful of fresh tarragon
    2 kale leaves

1. Core the apple and cut it into slices. Cut the cucumber into spears. Cut the peel off of the lemon half.

2. Juice the apple, cucumber, lemon, watercress, tarragon, and kale together, alternating the different kinds of produce as you juice (see page 23). Serve immediately.

Soothing Swizzle

Makes 12 to 16 ounces (355 to 475 ml)

B-complex vitamins and calcium can help to relieve tense muscles, and these nutrients are found in carrots. Apricots contain magnesium, which is known as both a stress-buster and a natural muscle relaxant.

> 2 apricots
> 6 carrots
> 4 celery stalks

1. Pit the apricots and cut them into slices.

2. Juice the apricots, carrots, and celery together. Serve immediately.

Slumber Elixir ▶

Makes 12 to 16 ounces (355 to 475 ml)

The essential oils in dill may have a calming effect on the body. Dill has been used since ancient times as a remedy for insomnia.

> 2 pears
> 4 celery stalks
> 1 cup (30 g) spinach leaves
> 1 small bunch of fresh dill

1. Core the pears and cut them into slices.

2. Juice the pears, celery, spinach, and dill together, alternating the different kinds of produce as you juice (see page 23). Serve immediately.

☞ **JUICY TIP**
If you're looking to improve your sleep, try drinking a calming juice an hour before bed and winding down with a warm bath.

CLEANSING
JUICES

Juicing daily is an efficient way to support your body's natural detoxification. Your body soaks in the nutrients without having to digest the fiber, allowing it to quickly use the nutrients to cleanse and heal. Here are some of my favorite blends for cleansing to keep your body in tip-top shape.

Spinach Power

Makes 12 to 16 ounces (355 to 475 ml)

Spinach juice is amazing at cleansing, reconstructing, and regenerating the intestinal tract.

> 4 large oranges
> 2 handfuls of spinach leaves
> 10 strawberries

1. Cut the peels off of the oranges and slice them into wedges.

2. Juice the oranges, spinach, and strawberries together, alternating the different kinds of produce as you juice (see page 23). Serve immediately.

✺ JUICY TIP
Strawberries are often used in cleansing because they are a mild tonic for the liver.

Celery Reviver

Makes 12 to 16 ounces (355 to 475 ml)

I love this blend for flushing toxins and for its well-rounded balance of nutrients.

> 2 tomatoes
> 1 lemon
> 4 carrots
> 5 celery stalks

1. Slice the tomatoes into wedges. Cut the peel off of the lemon and slice it in half.

2. Juice the tomatoes, lemon, carrots, and celery together. Serve immediately.

☞ JUICY TIP
Celery is beneficial for cleansing the body of carbon dioxide and of built-up deposits that accumulate in joints.

Herby Green Cleanser ▶

Makes 12 to 16 ounces (355 to 475 ml)

This blend has an amazingly fresh taste and is a strong internal cleanser.

    1 apple
    ½ of a cucumber
    1 cup (60 g) fresh parsley
    1 cup (16 g) fresh cilantro leaves
    3 sprigs of fresh dill
    1 cup (67 g) kale leaves
    3 celery stalks
    ½ cup (120 ml) coconut water

1. Core the apple and cut it into slices. Cut the cucumber into spears.

2. Juice the apple, cucumber, parsley, cilantro, dill, kale, and celery together, alternating the different kinds of produce as you juice (see page 23).

3. Add the coconut water and stir. Serve immediately.

☞ **JUICY TIP**
Because fresh herbs are so potent and medicinal in nature, they are a great addition to any detox regimen.

Acne Fix

Makes 12 to 16 ounces (355 to 475 ml)

Dandelion greens are used to cleanse the liver. Anyone with acne problems might benefit from a daily juice made from dandelion greens because when the liver is clean, it makes a difference in your skin.

> 1 small cucumber
> ½ of a lemon
> 1 handful of dandelion greens
> 6 carrots

1. Cut the cucumber into spears. Cut the peel off of the lemon half.

2. Juice the cucumber, lemon, dandelion greens, and carrots together, alternating the different kinds of produce as you juice (see page 23). Serve immediately.

Constipation Reliever

Makes 12 to 16 ounces (355 to 475 ml)

This classic blend helps to stimulate the peristaltic action of the intestines.

> 2 apples
> 2 pears
> ½ of a lime
> 1 large bunch of spinach leaves

1. Core the apples and cut them into slices. Core the pears and cut them into slices. Cut the peel off of the lime half.

2. Juice the apples, pears, lime, and spinach together, alternating the different kinds of produce as you juice (see page 23). Serve immediately.

🍐 JUICY TIP

Apples and pears are great sources of pectin, which helps digestion and cleanses the body of toxic waste by stimulating bowel activity.

◄ Daytime Detox

Makes 12 to 16 ounces (355 to 475 ml)

All lettuce greens contain chlorophyll, which helps to build red blood cell count and to detoxify the blood.

> 4 green apples
> 1 lemon
> 5 kale leaves
> 5 lettuce leaves
> ½-inch (1.3 cm) piece of fresh ginger

1. Core the apples and cut them into slices. Cut the peel off of the lemon and cut it in half.

2. Juice the apples, lemon, kale, lettuce leaves, and ginger together, alternating the different kinds of produce as you juice (see page 23) Serve immediately.

☞ **JUICY TIP**
Ginger acts as an expectorant, cleaning the sinus cavities of mucus and the lungs of phlegm.

Cranberry Vitality

Makes 12 to 16 ounces (355 to 475 ml)

Cranberries are known for helping to cleanse and heal the urinary canal. They contain quinine, an acid that penetrates the liver and then converts to hippuric acid, which removes uric acid and toxins from the bladder, kidneys, and prostate.

> 3 apples
> 1 large cucumber
> 2 cups (200 g) cranberries
> ½ of a lemon

1. Core the apples and cut them into slices. Cut the cucumber into spears.

2. Juice the apples, cucumber, cranberries, and lemon together, alternating the different kinds of produce as you juice (see page 23) Serve immediately.

🫘 **JUICY TIP**
Lemon peels, because of their bioflavonoid content, help to eradicate toxins in the body. If you're looking to cleanse your system on a daily basis, juice the peels of your lemons. Note that the oil in the peels adds a potent lemon flavor that can be overpowering, so use them in limited quantities.

Melon Balancer

Makes 12 to 16 ounces (355 to 475 ml)

Melons work well to detoxify the blood for alleviating a variety of health issues, especially when paired with apples and greens.

> 2 apples
> 2 cups (300 g) watermelon chunks
> 1 handful of green lettuce leaves

1. Core the apples and cut them into slices.

2. Juice the apples, watermelon, and lettuce leaves together, alternating the different kinds of produce as you juice (see page 23). Serve immediately.

> ◆ **JUICY TIP**
> Most fruit juices are particularly good for cleansing the kidneys and bowels.

Liver Elixir ▶

Makes 12 to 16 ounces (355 to 475 ml)

Especially good for liver cleansing, beets contain many vitamins and minerals that support detoxification. Add ¼ cup (60 ml) of coconut water, if you like, to enhance the nutrients and flavor.

> 1 beet
> 8 carrots

1. Cut the beet into quarters.

2. Juice the carrots and beet together. Serve immediately.

Carrot Kick

Makes 12 to 16 ounces (355 to 475 ml)

Carrots have a cleansing effect on the liver and the entire digestive system. They have anti-cancer properties and aid with problems associated with arthritis and gout.

> 6 carrots
> 1 small wedge of green cabbage
> 4 celery stalks
> 1 cup (165 g) fresh pineapple chunks

1. Juice the carrots, cabbage, celery, and pineapple together, alternating the different kinds of produce as you juice (see page 23). Serve immediately.

☞ **JUICY TIP**
Cabbage is the ultimate body detoxifier, but it is not very tasty on its own. Mix it with other vegetables and fruits to make it more palatable.

Gentle Detox Sipper

Makes 12 to 16 ounces (355 to 475 ml)

Cucumbers help your body to safely expel toxins that build up in your system. They are also used for acne problems and other skin issues, due to their detoxifying and anti-inflammatory properties.

> 2 cucumbers
> 1 apple
> 1 lemon
> 1 cup (300 g) grapes

1. Cut the cucumbers into spears. Core the apple and cut it into slices. Cut the peel off of the lemon and cut it in half.

2. Juice the cucumbers, apple, lemon, and grapes together. Serve immediately.

SLIMMING JUICES

Do you need some help shedding a few pounds or maintaining your weight? Juicing is not a quick fix for weight loss. However, some juice blends may assist your body in slimming down, curbing appetite, and de-bloating. Here are some of my favorite blends to help you meet your goals healthfully.

Skinny Mini Cocktail ▶

Makes 12 to 16 ounces (355 to 475 ml)

Watermelon is incredibly hydrating and cleansing. Adding celery and lemon just enhances the benefits.

> 1 lemon
> 3 cups (450 g) watermelon chunks
> 1 celery stalk

1. Cut the peel off of the lemon and cut it in half.

2. Juice the lemon, watermelon, and celery together. Serve immediately.

Lemon Alkalizer

Makes 12 to 16 ounces (355 to 475 ml)

Keeping your body alkaline is important to maintaining weight. Lemons and greens are excellent alkalizers, but they can be sour. The carrots add a wonderful creaminess to the recipe and take the edge off the tart lemon flavor.

> 1 lemon
> 6 carrots
> 2 romaine lettuce leaves

1. Cut the peel off of the lemon and cut it in half.

2. Juice the lemon, carrots, and romaine lettuce together, alternating the different kinds of produce as you juice (see page 23). Serve immediately.

> **🍋 JUICY TIP**
> Lemon is a gentle, natural laxative and diuretic. Because lemon possesses these properties, drinking lemon juice can help alleviate constipation and flush excess salt from your system.

Slimming Tonic

Makes 12 to 16 ounces (355 to 475 ml)

Many people believe that grapefruit is a food that's capable of melting off excess body fat naturally because it contains a fat-burning enzyme. Research from San Diego's Scripps Clinic indicates that adding grapefruit or its juice to your diet may help with weight loss and lower blood insulin levels.

> 2 apples
> 2 grapefruits

1. Core the apples and cut them into slices. Cut the peels off of the grapefruits, and slice them into wedges.

2. Juice the apples and grapefruits together, alternating the two kinds of produce as you juice (see page 23). Serve immediately.

Skinny Sipper

Makes 12 to 16 ounces (355 to 475 ml)

Apples and lemons have strong detoxifying properties that together may help to remove fat and toxins from the body.

>   2 apples
>   1 yellow bell pepper
>   1 lemon
>   1-inch (2.5 cm) piece of fresh ginger

1. Core the apples and cut them into slices. Cut the stem off the bell pepper and cut it into strips. Leave the peel on the lemon and cut it in half.

2. Juice the apples, bell pepper, lemon, and ginger together. Serve immediately.

Pineapple Hot Stuff ▶

Makes 12 to 16 ounces (355 to 475 ml)

Pineapple is great for dissolving mucus in the system, and the chile pepper may help to speed up metabolism. If you aren't sure you'll like the heat of the chile, only juice half of it.

>   1 lime
>   3 large carrots
>   2 cups (330 g) fresh pineapple chunks
>   1 red chile pepper or cayenne pepper
>   to taste

1. Cut the peel off of the lime and cut it in half.

2. Juice the lime, carrots, pineapple, and chile pepper together, alternating the different kinds of produce as you juice (see page 23). Serve immediately.

☞ **JUICY TIP**
Add fiber sources, such as psyllium husk or chia seeds, to your juice to help curb your appetite cravings.

Slender Swizzle ▶

Makes 12 to 16 ounces (355 to 475 ml)

I'll never forget how a few days before my wedding my mom broke out her juicer with this recipe to help her shed extra water weight. It worked like a charm.

   1 large cucumber
   1 apple
   1 lime
   2 celery stalks

1. Cut the cucumber into spears. Core the apple and cut it into slices. Leave the peel on the lime and cut it in half.

2. Juice the cucumber, apple, lime, and celery together. Serve immediately.

☞ **JUICY TIP**
Celery and cucumbers act as diuretics and will aid your body in releasing excess water.

Lean Beauty Punch

Makes 12 to 16 ounces (355 to 475 ml)

This tasty low-cal blend keeps cravings in check and helps to eliminate excess water weight at the same time.

> 1 small to medium cucumber
> 5 large carrots
> 3 celery stalks

1. Cut the cucumber into spears.

2. Juice the cucumber, carrots, and celery together. Serve immediately.

Green Detoxer

Makes 12 to 16 ounces (355 to 475 ml)

Clean out toxins and fat with this tasty combination. It's a great way to start your morning.

> 1 apple
> 1 zucchini
> 5 celery stalks
> 3 large kale leaves

1. Core the apple and cut it into slices. Cut the zucchini into spears.

2. Juice the apple, zucchini, celery, and kale together, alternating the different kinds of produce as you juice (see page 23). Serve immediately.

☞ **JUICY TIP**
Compounds in celery have been shown to reduce water retention. In addition, celery's high water content can help flush out excessive amounts of sodium.

Tomato Trim-Down

Makes 12 to 16 ounces (355 to 475 ml)

This sweet tomato blend will make you swoon. It's great for an afternoon snack to help curb your appetite.

2 tomatoes
1 yellow bell pepper
1 small to medium cucumber

1. Cut the tomatoes into slices. Cut the stem off the bell pepper and cut it into strips. Cut the cucumber into spears.

2. Juice the tomatoes, bell pepper, and cucumber together. Serve immediately.

🖒 **JUICY TIP**
Bell pepper is a smart way to add sweetness to a recipe without adding a lot of sugar, which can sabotage a diet.

Skinny Apple Cleanser ▶

Makes 12 to 16 ounces (355 to 475 ml)

The pectin in apples remains in the juice and helps to sweep away toxins and fat from your body.

2 apples
1 pear
½ of a cucumber
7 celery stalks

1. Core the apples and cut them into slices. Core the pear and cut it into slices. Cut the cucumber half into spears.

2. Juice the apples, pear, cucumber, and celery together. Serve immediately.

Flat Belly Blast

Makes 12 to 16 ounces (355 to 475 ml)

This simple recipe combines the fat-burning properties of grapefruit with the cleansing properties of lime.

>   3 medium grapefruits
>   1 lime
>   5 strawberries

1. Cut the peels off of the grapefruits and slice them into wedges. Cut the lime in half, but leave the peel on, if you like.

2. Juice the grapefruits, lime, and strawberries together, alternating the different kinds of produce as you juice (see page 23). Serve immediately.

Super Slimmer

Makes 12 to 16 ounces (355 to 475 ml)

This blend will help you shed excess water weight and cleanse your liver.

>   4 apples
>   1 lemon
>   1 small to medium cucumber
>   5 celery stalks

1. Core the apples and cut them into slices. Leave the peel on the lemon and cut it in half. Cut the cucumber into spears.

2. Juice the apples, lemon, cucumber, and celery, alternating the different kinds of produce as you juice (see page 23). Serve immediately.

☞ **JUICY TIP**
Celery juice is extremely low in calories. Drinking it throughout the day will help you feel full and reduce your cravings for fattening snacks.

Cantaloupe Fat Buster

Makes 12 to 16 ounces (355 to 475 ml)

This is a classic and tasty recipe for removing fat and slimming down.

> 7 large carrots
> 2 cups (320 g) cantaloupe chunks

1. Juice the carrots and cantaloupe together. Serve immediately.

Spicy Pear Slim-Down

Makes 12 to 16 ounces (355 to 475 ml)

The taste of this blend can't be beat. It also may help with improved digestion and decreased bloating.

> 2 pears
> 7 celery stalks
> 1-inch (2.5 cm) piece of fresh ginger

1. Core the pears and cut them into slices.

2. Juice the pears, celery, and ginger together. Serve immediately.

Metabolism Booster

Makes 12 to 16 ounces (355 to 475 ml)

This combination of nutrients is sure to help speed up your internal fire.

> 1 cucumber
> 1 lemon
> ½ of a beet
> 5 carrots
> ½ of a jalapeño or other green chile pepper
> 3 celery stalks

1. Cut the cucumber into spears. Cut the peel off of the lemon and slice it into wedges. Cut the beet into quarters.

2. Juice the cucumber, lemon, beet, carrot, chile pepper, and celery together. Serve immediately.

☞ **JUICY TIP**
Cucumber's high water content makes it one of the great juices for controlling belly bloating.

JUICE
SHOTS

Juice shots are small shots of potent juices made to boost your health and well-being. They are formulated with fruits, vegetables, and superfoods known for their unique nutritional, healing, and medicinal properties. They are typically consumed for strengthened immunity, glowing skin, enhanced circulation, or energy. You can find them in almost any juice bar, but these powerful shooters are super easy to make in your own kitchen.

Pineapple Wheatgrass Shot

Makes 1 shot

Wheatgrass is an amazing food that has been used medicinally for centuries. Its healing properties are hard to beat. Many people don't like the taste of a straight-up wheatgrass shot but want the benefits, so mixing it with pineapple is a perfect solution.

1 cup (165 g) fresh pineapple chunks
1 handful of wheatgrass

1. Juice the pineapple and wheatgrass together. (If you have one, juice the wheatgrass in a wheatgrass juicer or masticating juicer separately to get the maximum amount of liquid from the grass.) Serve immediately.

Super Greens Shot

Makes 1 shot

This super shot will help alkalize and cleanse your entire body. You'll need a special juicer for the wheatgrass.

1 apple
A few handfuls of wheatgrass
1 teaspoon spirulina powder
1 teaspoon chlorella powder

1. Core the apple and cut it into slices.

2. Juice the apple and wheatgrass together. (If you have one, juice the wheatgrass in a wheatgrass juicer or masticating juicer separately to get the maximum amount of liquid from the grass.)

3. Pour the juice into a small glass and add the spirulina and chlorella powders. Stir to combine. Serve immediately.

☞ **JUICY TIP**
A strong green shot like this can be overwhelming if you've never had anything like it before. It's an acquired taste and taken mainly for its health benefits— it is a strong detoxifier.

Red Beet Ginger Shot ▶

Makes 1 shot

Beets are a blood builder and will help boost oxygen supply to the blood. This shot will provide the body with increased energy and stamina.

1 red beet
1-inch (2.5 cm) piece of fresh ginger

1. Cut the beet into quarters.

2. Juice the beet and ginger together. Serve immediately.

> 🥕 **JUICY TIP**
> It's not recommended to have beet juice alone except in a small quantity, like a shot. Beets are powerful cleansers.

Ginger Shot

Makes 1 shot

Ginger supports healthy digestion and immunity. It has antinausea, anti-inflammatory, and antioxidant compounds. You'll find this pungent juice invigorating, and it might give you an immediate boost of energy.

4 to 6 (10 to 15 cm) inches of fresh ginger

1. Juice the ginger in your juicer. Serve immediately.

Cold and Flu Shot

Makes 1 shot

High in vitamin C, this shot will boost your immunity to keep colds away or under control.

½ of an orange
1 carrot
1-inch (2.5 cm) piece of fresh ginger

1. Cut the peel off of the orange half.

2. Juice the orange, carrot, and ginger together. Serve immediately.

Chile Lime Shot

Makes 1 shot

Lime peels have antibacterial properties, and chile peppers are great for improved circulation and cancer prevention. This shot is not for everyone, but if you can take the heat, you'll love it.

1 lime
1 mild red chile pepper

1. Leave the peel on the lime and cut it in half.

2. Juice the lime and chile together. Serve immediately.

◀ Aloe Vera Apple Shot

Makes 1 shot

Aloe vera is fantastic for the entire digestive system and is especially good to consume when you have stomach troubles.

> 1 apple
> 1 aloe leaf

1. Core the apple and cut it into slices. Cut open the aloe leaf and scrape out the gel with a spoon into a small glass.

2. Juice the apple.

3. Mix the aloe gel with the apple juice in the glass and stir to combine. Serve immediately.

> ☞ **JUICY TIP**
> Aloe doesn't have much flavor, and it is very thick. It's easier to consume when it's mixed with apple juice, carrot juice, or lemon juice.

Red Beet Lemon Shot

Makes 1 shot

This shot will invigorate your whole system and support your liver.

> 1 lemon
> 1 beet

1. Cut the peel off of the lemon and slice it into wedges. Cut the beet into quarters.

2. Juice the lemon and beet together. Serve immediately.

Spirulina Apple Shot

Makes 1 shot

Spirulina is great for cleansing and for thyroid support. While you can't juice it, you can find it easily in powdered form for mixing into juices or water.

> 1 large apple
> 1 tablespoon (17 g) spirulina powder

1. Core the apple and cut it into slices.

2. Juice the apple and pour into a small glass. Add the spirulina powder and stir to combine. Serve immediately.

Turmeric Lemon Shot

Makes 1 shot

Turmeric root contains anti-aging, anti-inflammatory, and immune-building properties.

> 1 large lemon
> 4 inches (10 cm) of fresh turmeric or 1 teaspoon ground turmeric

1. Leave the peel on the lemon and slice it into wedges.

2. Juice the lemon and the fresh turmeric together. If you don't have fresh turmeric, juice the lemon, add the ground turmeric, and stir to combine. Serve immediately.

Lemon Garlic Shot

Makes 1 shot

If you're under the weather, this juice might help build your immunity and get you back on your feet. It's also great for relieving nasal congestion.

> 1 large lemon
> 1 garlic clove

1. Cut the peel off of the lemon and slice it into wedges.

2. Juice the lemon and garlic together. Serve immediately.

☞ **JUICY TIP**
Garlic juice doesn't leave the best aftertaste, but the lemon will help minimize the effect. Garlic is known to help strengthen the immune system and to help keep the heart healthy.

◀ Detox Shot

Makes 1 shot

This blend will stimulate your body to cleanse and detoxify. Consider adding mint to this recipe to further enhance its detox power.

½ of an apple
¼ of a beet
1 small wedge of red cabbage

1. Core the apple and cut it into slices.

2. Juice the apple, beet, and red cabbage together. Serve immediately.

◀ Ginger, Lemon, and Cayenne Shot

Makes 1 shot

Ginger, lemon, and cayenne together create a cleansing mix that detoxifies and helps to boost metabolism. As you kick back this shot, you'll feel right away how warming and energizing it is to your body.

> 1 large lemon
> 2-inch (5 cm) piece of fresh ginger
> Pinch of cayenne pepper

1. Cut the peel off of the lemon and cut it in half.

2. Juice the lemon and ginger together.

3. Pour into a small glass and add a pinch of cayenne pepper. Stir to combine. Serve immediately.

Flu Buster Shot

Makes 1 shot

Keep your immunity strong and the flu bugs at bay with this blend.

> 1 large lemon
> 2-inch (5 cm) piece of fresh ginger
> 1 teaspoon Echinacea tincture

1. Cut the peel off of the lemon and cut it in half.

2. Juice the lemon and ginger together.

3. Pour into a glass, add the Echinacea tincture, and stir to combine. Serve immediately.

Red Cabbage Apple Shot

Makes 1 shot

Cabbage is a disinfectant for the colon and contains sulforaphane, which is known for helping the body fight diseases. Fresh cabbage is very strong in flavor, so it's best to mix it with water and other juices.

1 apple
1 large wedge of red cabbage
¼ cup (60 ml) cold water

1. Core the apple and cut it into slices.

2. Juice the apple and cabbage together.

3. Pour into a small glass and mix with the water. Serve immediately.

Turmeric Cherry Shot ▶

Makes 1 shot

Turmeric and cherry are loaded with anti-inflammatory compounds that may help ease joint pain and relieve gout.

1 cup (155 g) cherries
4 inches (10 cm) fresh turmeric or 1 teaspoon ground turmeric

1. Pit the cherries.

2. Juice the cherries and the fresh turmeric together. If you don't have fresh turmeric, add the ground turmeric to the juiced cherries and stir to combine. Serve immediately.

Wellness Shot

Makes 1 shot

This blend is a quick way to boost overall immunity and wellness. It's a powerful blend but not as strong as some other shots, making this one good for kids.

½ of a lemon
1 celery stalk
½ of an apple
1-inch (2.5 cm) piece of fresh ginger

1. Cut the peel off of the lemon half.

2. Juice the lemon, celery, apple, and ginger together. Serve immediately.

Kale Apple Shot

Makes 1 shot

Kale promotes eye health and is a great source of copper, potassium, iron, manganese, and phosphorous. The apple makes it easier to digest.

1 apple
6 kale leaves

1. Core the apple and cut it into slices.

2. Juice the apple slices and kale together, alternating the the two kinds of produce as you juice (see page 23). Serve immediately.

☞ **JUICY TIP**
When juicing kale shots, you'll want the juiciest kale possible. Choose varieties like lacinato or curly kale and be sure to use the stems, too.

Immune Booster Shot

Makes 1 shot

If you're looking for a quick way to boost your immune system, this is the juice for you. Oregano oil is highly antibacterial.

    1 lemon
    1-inch (2.5 cm) piece of fresh ginger
    Pinch of cayenne pepper
    2 drops oregano oil

1. Cut the peel off of the lemon and cut it in half.

2. Juice the lemon and ginger together.

3. Pour into a small glass and add the cayenne pepper and oregano oil. Stir to combine and serve immediately.

Kale, Pear, and Turmeric Shot

Makes 1 shot

This power-packed punch is an immunity builder and has anti-inflammatory properties.

    1 pear
    2 kale leaves
    2-inch (5 cm) piece of fresh turmeric or
      1 teaspoon ground turmeric

1. Core the pear and cut it into slices.

2. Juice the pear, kale, and fresh turmeric together, alternating the different kinds of produce as you juice (see page 23). If using ground turmeric instead of fresh, mix it in with the pear and kale juice. Serve immediately.

PARTY
PUNCHES

Are you in need of the perfect drink to serve a crowd? Prepare your guests a tasty, healthful punch full of nutrients. I crafted these juice punches to please friends and family and win them over on making fresh juice, whether they're already juice fans or not. And because real juice produces vibrantly hued drinks, these punches make a wonderful presentation. Break out the punch bowl. It's time for a party!

Lemon, Apple, and Beet Punch

Makes 1 small pitcher (32 to 48 ounces, or 950 ml to 1.4 L)

One part sour and one part sweet, this beet lemonade is always tasty and is very economical to make.

- 6 apples
- 5 lemons
- 2 red beets
- 1 cup (235 ml) cold water

1. Core the apples and cut them into slices. Cut the peels off of the lemons and cut them in half. Cut the beets into quarters.

2. Juice the apples, lemons, and beets together.

3. Pour into a pitcher and add the water. Stir to combine. Serve immediately.

Strawberry, Lime, and Pear Punch

Makes 1 small pitcher (32 to 48 ounces, or 950 ml to 1.4 L)

This punch is a beautiful rose color and has a subtle sweetness that most people enjoy.

- 6 pears
- 4 limes
- 1 pound (455 g) strawberries
- 1 cup (235 ml) cold water

1. Core the pears and cut them into slices. Cut the peels off of the limes and cut them in half.

2. Juice the pears, limes, and strawberries together, alternating the different kinds of produce as you juice (see page 23).

3. Pour into a pitcher and add the water. Stir to combine. Serve immediately.

☞ **JUICY TIP**
Serve your juice punch straight from a punch bowl with ice cubes on the side. Putting ice into the punch will dilute the mixture and might jeopardize the flavor.

◀ Orange Mango Punch

Makes 1 small pitcher (32 to 48 ounces, or 950 ml to 1.4 L)

This mango-spiked juice is perfect for any occasion.

> 8 oranges
> 3 mangoes
> 1 cup (235 ml) cold water

1. Peel the oranges and slice them into wedges. Cut the peels off of the mangoes and discard the pits. Cut the flesh into spears or chunks.

2. Juice the oranges and mangoes together.

3. Pour into a pitcher and add the water. Stir to combine. Serve immediately.

☞ **JUICY TIP**
If you want to make any punch alcoholic, add Champagne, vodka, or your spirit of choice to the blend.

◀ Grapefruit Melon Punch

Makes 1 small pitcher (32 to 48 ounces, or 950 ml to 1.4 L)

I find this to be the ultimate crowd-pleasing brunch punch.

4 grapefruits
1 mini watermelon or about ¼ of a large watermelon
1 cup (235 ml) cold water (optional)

1. Cut the peels off of the grapefruits and slice them into wedges. Cut the watermelon into chunks or spears.

2. Juice the grapefruit and watermelon together.

3. Pour into a pitcher. Add the water if you'd like a more diluted punch, but it's not necessary. Stir to combine. Serve immediately.

Cucumber, Grape, and Kale Punch

Makes 1 small pitcher (32 to 48 ounces, or 950 ml to 1.4 L)

If you know your crowd won't mind a hint of green juice, this refreshing blend is perfect. It's a great option for a fitness-related event.

2 large cucumbers
6 cups (900 g) green grapes
4 kale leaves
1 cup (235 ml) cold water

1. Cut the cucumbers into spears.

2. Juice the cucumbers, grapes, and kale together, alternating the different kinds of produce as you juice (see page 23).

3. Pour into a pitcher and add the water. Stir to combine. Serve immediately.

Pineapple, Mango, and Carrot Punch

Makes 1 small pitcher (32 to 48 ounces, or 950 ml to 1.4 L)

This tropical and healthful combination is always popular.

2 fresh pineapples
2 mangoes
6 carrots
1 cup (235 ml) cold water

1. Cut the pineapples into spears. Cut the peel off of the mangoes and discard the pits. Cut the flesh into spears or chunks.

2. Juice the pineapples, mangoes, and carrots together.

3. Pour into a pitcher and add the water. Stir to combine. Serve immediately.

☞ **JUICY TIP**
Do you prefer sparkling party punches? Add sparkling mineral water instead of still water to make it fizzy.

Red Beet, Orange, and Apple Punch

Makes 1 small pitcher (32 to 48 ounces, or 950 ml to 1.4 L)

While this juice is mostly apple and orange with a little bit of beet, it is a gorgeous deep pink color. It's perfect for a female-themed event.

8 oranges
2 apples
1 red beet
1 cup (235 ml) cold water

1. Cut the peels off of the oranges and slice them into wedges. Core the apples and cut them into slices. Cut the beet into quarters.

2. Juice the oranges, apples, and beet together.

3. Pour into a pitcher and add the water. Stir to combine. Serve immediately.

◀ Carrot, Lemon, and Pineapple Punch

Makes 1 small pitcher (32 to 48 ounces, or 950 ml to 1.4 L)

Carrots make this juice blend very orange in color, but it's also sweet and incredibly tasty.

2 lemons
1 fresh pineapple
10 carrots
1 cup (235 ml) cold water

1. Cut the peel off of the lemons and cut them in half. Cut the pineapple into spears.

2. Juice the lemons, pineapple, and carrots together.

3. Pour into a pitcher and add the water. Stir to combine. Serve immediately.

Grapefruit Grape Punch ▶

Makes 1 small pitcher (32 to 48 ounces, or 950 ml to 1.4 L)

This blend is sweet and hydrating, making it good for warmer outdoor parties or a large picnic.

5 grapefruits
2 cups (300 g) green grapes
1 cup (235 ml) cold water (optional)

1. Cut the peels off of the grapefruits and slice them into wedges.

2. Juice the grapefruit and grapes together.

3. Pour into a pitcher. Add the water if you'd like a more diluted punch, but it's not necessary. Stir to combine. Serve immediately.

Orange Pineapple Punch

Makes 1 small pitcher (32 to 48 ounces, or 950 ml to 1.4 L)

Great for a summertime pool party, this one is a crowd favorite.

> 6 oranges
> 1 fresh pineapple
> 1 cup (235 ml) cold water

1. Cut the peels off of the oranges and slice them into wedges. Cut the pineapple into spears.

2. Juice the oranges and pineapple together.

3. Pour into a pitcher and add the water. Stir to combine. Serve immediately.

☞ JUICY TIP

If you're not into punch bowls or pitchers, fill a glass of juice for each person at your event and serve everyone individually. You're likely to waste less punch this way.

Lemon, Lime, and Pineapple Punch

Makes 1 small pitcher (32 to 48 ounces, or 950 ml to 1.4 L)

This tart punch reminds me of the popular sherbets and bottled sodas that have the same flavors, but this is way healthier. Use sparkling water if you want to make this a fizzy drink.

> 2 fresh pineapples
> 2 limes
> 1 lemon
> 1 cup (235 ml) cold water

1. Cut the pineapples into spears. Cut the peels off of the limes and lemon and slice them into wedges.

2. Juice the pineapple, limes, and lemon together.

3. Pour into a pitcher and add the water. Stir to combine. Serve immediately.

Green Grape Celery Punch

Makes 1 small pitcher (32 to 48 ounces, or 950 ml to 1.4 L)

The celery balances out the sweet grape juice nicely. It's a great choice for kids' parties where adults might want a sip, too.

> 6 cups (900 g) green grapes
> 8 celery stalks
> 1 cup (235 ml) cold water

1. Juice the grapes and celery together.

2. Pour into a pitcher and add the water. Stir to combine. Serve immediately.

Watermelon, Raspberry, and Lemon Punch

Makes 1 small pitcher (32 to 48 ounces, or 950 ml to 1.4 L)

Not one person at your party wouldn't like this refreshing and beautiful punch. It also is less sweet than some of the other punches in this chapter.

> 1 mini watermelon or about ¼ of
>   a large watermelon
> 3 lemons
> 1 cup (125 g) raspberries
> 1 cup (235 ml) cold water

1. Cut the watermelon into chunks or spears. Cut the peels off of the lemons and slice them into wedges.

2. Juice the watermelon, lemon, and raspberries together, alternating the different kinds of produce as you juice (see page 23).

3. Pour into a pitcher and add the water. Stir to combine. Serve immediately.

Cranberry, Apple, and Lime Punch

Makes 1 small pitcher (32 to 48 ounces, or 950 ml to 1.4 L)

This combination is tart and sweet and really flavorful.

> 10 apples
> 4 limes, peeled
> 2 cups (200 g) cranberries
> 1 cup (235 ml) cold water

1. Core the apples and cut them into slices.

2. Juice the apples, limes, and cranberries together, alternating the different kinds of produce as you juice (see page 23).

3. Pour into a pitcher and add the water. Stir to combine. Serve immediately.

☞ **JUICY TIP**

Because fresh juice doesn't store well, make it no more than an hour before an event to ensure freshness. When making punch with apple or pear, make it just before the event. These fruits oxidize quickly, so the juice will become browner the longer it sits out. Or you can opt for melon and citrus punches instead.

Blackberry Pineapple Punch

Makes 1 small pitcher (32 to 48 ounces, or 950 ml to 1.4 L)

This pineapple-berry blend is an amazing dessert drink.

> 2 fresh pineapples
> 2 cups (290 g) blackberries
> 1 cup (235 ml) cold water

1. Cut the pineapples into spears.

2. Juice the pineapples and blackberries together, alternating the different kinds of produce as you juice (see page 23).

3. Pour into a pitcher and add the water. Stir to combine. Serve immediately.

◄ Lemon, Lime, Pineapple, and Raspberry Punch

Makes 1 small pitcher (32 to 48 ounces, or 950 ml to 1.4 L)

This low-sugar punch has just a hint of sweetness with the addition of a pineapple. It's a beautiful flamingo pink color and will not disappoint.

> 1 lemon
> 1 lime
> 1 fresh pineapple
> 1 cup (125 g) raspberries
> 1 cup (235 ml) cold water

1. Cut the peels off of the lemon and lime and slice them into wedges. Cut the pineapple into spears.

2. Juice the lemon, lime, pineapple, and raspberries together, alternating the different kinds of produce as you juice (see page 23).

3. Pour into a pitcher and add the water. Stir to combine. Serve immediately.

Watermelon, Cucumber, and Mint Punch

Makes 1 small pitcher (32 to 48 ounces, or 950 ml to 1.4 L)

If you are hosting or bringing something to a group picnic or an outdoor party, consider this light and easy mix.

> 1 mini watermelon or about ¼ of a large watermelon
> 2 cucumbers
> 5 sprigs of fresh mint
> 1 cup (235 ml) cold water

1. Cut the watermelon into chunks or spears. Cut the cucumbers into spears.

2. Juice the watermelon, cucumbers, and mint together, alternating the different kinds of produce as you juice (see page 23).

3. Pour into a pitcher and add the water. Stir to combine. Serve immediately.

> ☞ **JUICY TIP**
> Be sure to keep your punch chilled to keep it fresh longer.

Pineapple Cucumber Punch

Makes 1 small pitcher (32 to 48 ounces, or 950 ml to 1.4 L)

This simple punch has been a hit every time I have served it. People always ask for more, and I can never seem to make enough!

    5 cucumbers
    1 fresh pineapple
    1 cup (235 ml) cold water

1. Cut the cucumbers into spears. Cut the pineapple into spears.

2. Juice the pineapple and cucumbers together.

3. Pour into a pitcher and add the water. Stir to combine. Serve immediately.

Peach, Lemon, and Cucumber Punch

Makes 1 small pitcher (32 to 48 ounces, or 950 ml to 1.4 L)

This cooling blend is a classy choice for an office lunch. Add coconut water instead of plain water, if you like, for a sweeter flavor.

    8 peaches
    5 large cucumbers
    3 lemons
    1 cup (235 ml) cold water

1. Pit the peaches and cut them into slices. Cut the cucumbers into spears. Cut the peels off of the lemons and slice them into wedges.

2. Juice the peaches, cucumbers, and lemons together.

3. Pour into a pitcher and add the water. Stir to combine. Serve immediately.

Orange Cranberry Punch

Makes 1 small pitcher (32 to 48 ounces, or 950 ml to 1.4 L)

This fall-inspired punch is great around the holidays for brunch.

10 oranges
2 cups (200 g) cranberries
1 cup (235 ml) cold water

1. Cut the peels off of the oranges and slice them into wedges.

2. Juice the oranges and cranberries together, alternating the two kinds of produce as you juice (see page 23).

3. Pour into a pitcher and add the water. Stir to combine. Serve immediately.

JUICE
SODAS

If you're the type of person who likes sodas, spritzers, and other bubbly drinks, you're going to love these juice sodas. Bubbles add a little pizzazz to any juice—and I'm not talking the alcoholic kind. Carbonated water combines with fresh juice to create fun and tasty juice sodas that will replace those unhealthy soft drinks for good. Both kids and your party guests will find any of these sodas to be a tasty, refreshing treat.

Pineapple Lime Soda

Makes 12 to 16 ounces (355 to 475 ml)

The sour lime and sweet pineapple mix beautifully together in this fruit soda.

½ of a lime
2 cups (330 g) fresh pineapple chunks
½ cup (120 ml) cold sparkling water

1. Slice the lime half into wedges, leaving the peel on.

2. Juice the lime and pineapple together.

3. Pour the juice into a large glass and add the sparkling water. Serve immediately.

Apple Pomegranate Soda

Makes 12 to 16 ounces (355 to 475 ml)

Pomegranates are filled with antioxidants. Consume this soda to help your body fight free radicals and keep you looking young.

1 apple
1 pomegranate
½ cup (120 ml) cold sparkling water

1. Core the apple and cut it into slices. Cut the pomegranate in half. Remove the arils with your hands in a bowl of water. Drain the water and discard the pith and peel.

2. Juice the apple and pomegranate arils together.

3. Pour the juice into a large glass and add the sparkling water. Serve immediately.

☞ **JUICY TIP**
Never juice the white pith of the pomegranate. It contains compounds that are toxic and may make you sick if ingested.

Sweet Orange Soda ▶

Makes 12 to 16 ounces (355 to 475 ml)

This soda doesn't taste exactly like store-bought orange soda. It's better!

> 1 orange
> ½ of an apple
> ½ cup (120 ml) sparkling water

1. Peel the orange and slice it into wedges. Core the apple half and cut it into slices.

2. Juice the orange and apple together.

3. Pour the juice into a large glass and add the sparkling water. Serve immediately.

Grape Peach Soda

Makes 12 to 16 ounces (355 to 475 ml)

When fresh peaches are in season, grab them at your local farmer's market and make this perfect dessert-like soda.

> 1 peach
> 1 cup (150 g) green grapes
> ½ cup (120 ml) cold sparkling water

1. Pit the peach and cut it into slices.

2. Juice the peach and grapes together.

3. Pour the juice into a large glass and add the sparkling water. Serve immediately.

Pear Apple Soda

Makes 12 to 16 ounces (355 to 475 ml)

Light, sweet, and refreshing, this soda will please anyone who isn't yet familiar with natural-juice sodas.

> 1 pear
> 1 apple
> ½ cup (120 ml) cold sparkling water

1. Core the pear and apple and cut them into slices.

2. Juice the pear and apple slices together.

3. Pour the juice into a large glass and add the sparkling water. Serve immediately.

Sour Apple Soda

Makes 12 to 16 ounces (355 to 475 ml)

If you were ever into sour apple candies when you were a kid, this soda might bring you back in time.

> 1 large apple
> 1 lime
> ½ cup (120 ml) cold sparkling water

1. Core the apple and cut it into slices. Slice the lime into wedges, leaving the peel on.

2. Juice the apple and lime together.

3. Pour the juice into a large glass and add the sparkling water. Serve immediately.

> **JUICY TIP**
> If you like sweeter juice sodas, add an extra apple or pear to the recipe.

Cranberry, Apple, and Grape Soda

Makes 12 to 16 ounces (355 to 475 ml)

Here's the classic cran-apple-grape juice turned into a fizzy delight. Who could resist this?

> 1 apple
> 1 cup (150 g) red grapes
> ½ cup (50 g) cranberries
> ½ cup (120 ml) sparkling water

1. Core the apple and cut it into slices.

2. Juice the apple, grapes, and cranberries together, alternating the different kinds of produce as you juice (see page 23).

3. Pour the juice into a large glass and add the sparkling water. Serve immediately.

Pineapple Soda ▶

Makes 12 to 16 ounces (355 to 475 ml)

Perfect for sipping by the pool, this sweet soda will complete your day.

> 2 cups (330 g) fresh pineapple chunks
> ½ cup (120 ml) cold sparkling water

1. Juice the pineapple chunks.

2. Pour the juice into a glass and add the sparkling water. Serve immediately.

☞ **JUICY TIP**
Any variety of sparkling water—seltzer water, club soda, or sparkling mineral water—will work well in these recipes.

Strawberry Orange Soda

Makes 12 to 16 ounces (355 to 475 ml)

I find this beautifully pink drink to be a bright spot in my day. It's also perfect for cool summer nights on the front porch.

1 large orange
7 strawberries
½ cup (120 ml) sparkling water

1. Remove the peel from the orange and slice it into wedges.

2. Juice the orange and strawberries together, alternating the two kinds of produce as you juice (see page 23).

3. Pour the juice into a large glass and add the sparkling water. Serve immediately.

Blueberry Grape Soda

Makes 12 to 16 ounces (355 to 475 ml)

I just love this combination of grapes and berries together. You could use green grapes, but red grapes make for a more attractive presentation.

2 cups (300 g) red grapes
1 cup (145 g) blueberries
½ cup (120 ml) cold sparkling water

1. Juice the grapes and blueberries and together, alternating the two kinds of produce as you juice (see page 23).

2. Pour the juice into a large glass and add the sparkling water. Serve immediately.

☞ **JUICY TIP**
Juice sodas don't keep well in the refrigerator because the carbonation dissipates. It's best to only make what you can drink immediately.

Tart Apple Soda

Makes 12 to 16 ounces (355 to 475 ml)

A little sweet and a little tart, this combination is light and refreshing.

1 apple
1 lemon
½ cup (120 ml) cold sparkling water

1. Core the apple and cut it into slices. Cut the peel off of the lemon and cut it in half.

2. Juice the apple and lemon together.

3. Pour the juice into a large glass and add the sparkling water. Serve immediately.

Grape Apple Soda

Makes 12 to 16 ounces (355 to 475 ml)

This classic is sure to be a winner with the kids!

1 apple
2 cups (300 g) green grapes
½ cup (120 ml) cold sparkling water

1. Core the apple and cut it into slices.

2. Juice the apple and grapes together, alternating the two kinds of produce as you juice (see page 23).

3. Pour the juice into a large glass and add the sparkling water. Serve immediately.

Sour Cherry Soda

Makes 12 to 16 ounces (355 to 475 ml)

If cherry season is on your horizon, get ready to try this! A hint of lime with the sweetness of cherries is enough to make anyone smile. If you'd like this soda to be a little sweeter, add an apple.

20 cherries
2 small limes
½ cup (120 ml) cold sparkling water

1. Pit the cherries. Cut the peels off of the limes and cut them in half.

2. Juice the cherries and limes together, alternating the two kinds of produce as you juice (see page 23).

3. Pour the juice into a large glass and add the sparkling water. Serve immediately.

Strawberry Cherry Soda ▶

Makes 12 to 16 ounces (355 to 475 ml)

This red sparkler is sweet and nostalgic.

1 pear
10 cherries
7 strawberries
½ cup (120 ml) cold sparkling water

1. Core the pear and cut it into slices. Pit the cherries.

2. Juice the pear, cherries, and strawberries, alternating the different kinds of produce as you juice (see page 23).

3. Pour the juice into a large glass and add the sparkling water. Serve immediately.

Raspberry Lemon Soda

Makes 12 to 16 ounces (355 to 475 ml)

Raspberries add a special zing to this juice soda. It's one of my favorites.

> 1 apple
> ½ of a lemon
> 1 cup (125 g) raspberries
> ½ cup (120 ml) cold sparkling water

1. Core the apple and cut it into slices. Remove the peel from the lemon half and cut it in half.

2. Juice the apple, lemon, and raspberries together, alternating the two kinds of produce as you juice (see page 23).

3. Pour the juice into a large glass and add the sparkling water. Serve immediately.

Spicy Apple Ginger Soda

Makes 12 to 16 ounces (355 to 475 ml)

This spicy soda is great to have if you're feeling ill and a little nauseous. It might help to calm your stomach.

> 2 apples
> 1 celery stalk
> 1-inch (2.5 cm) piece of fresh ginger
> ½ cup (120 ml) cold sparkling water

1. Core the apples and cut them into slices.

2. Juice the apples, celery, and ginger together.

3. Pour the juice into a large glass and add the sparkling water. Serve immediately.

Spicy Orange Mango Soda

Makes 12 to 16 ounces (355 to 475 ml)

The ginger in this orange-mango soda adds a nice heat to the overall flavor.

> 1 mango
> 1 orange
> 1-inch (2.5 cm) piece of fresh ginger
> ½ cup (120 ml) cold sparkling water

1. Cut the peel off of the mango and discard the pit. Cut the flesh into spears or chunks. Cut the peel off of the orange and slice it into wedges.

2. Juice the mango, orange, and ginger together.

3. Pour the juice into a large glass and add the sparkling water. Serve immediately.

Grapefruit Orange Soda ▶

Makes 12 to 16 ounces (355 to 475 ml)

Sour grapefruit meets sweet orange in this soda. It couldn't be a better combination.

> 1 grapefruit
> 1 orange
> ½ cup (120 ml) cold sparkling water

1. Cut the peel off of the grapefruit and slice it into wedges. Cut the peel off of the orange and cut it into slices.

2. Juice the grapefruit and orange together.

3. Pour the juice into a large glass and add the sparkling water. Serve immediately.

◄ Green Grape Soda

Makes 12 to 16 ounces (355 to 475 ml)

Apples and celery add a nice, not too sweet, light flavor to your typical grape juice soda.

> 1 green apple
> 1 cup (150 g) green grapes
> 1 celery stalk
> ½ cup (120 ml) cold sparkling water

1. Core the apple and cut it into slices.

2. Juice the apple, grapes, and celery together.

3. Pour the juice into a large glass and add the sparkling water. Serve immediately.

☞ **JUICY TIP**
Celery balances out the sweetness of fruit sodas.

Kiwi Pear Soda

Makes 12 to 16 ounces (355 to 475 ml)

Kiwifruit and pear are an amazing couple in this sweet-and-sour fizzy drink.

> 3 kiwifruits
> 1 pear
> ½ cup (120 ml) cold sparkling water

1. Peel the kiwis and cut them in half. Core the pear and cut it into slices.

2. Juice the kiwis and pear together.

3. Pour the juice into a large glass and add the sparkling water. Serve immediately.

Pineapple Raspberry Soda

Makes 12 to 16 ounces (355 to 475 ml)

I am in love with pink raspberries—they make any juice more fun. You'll love this sweet and fruity combination.

2 cups (330 g) fresh pineapple chunks
1 cup (125 g) raspberries
½ cup (120 ml) cold sparkling water

1. Juice the pineapple and raspberries together, alternating the two kinds of produce as you juice (see page 23).

2. Pour the juice into a large glass and add the sparking water. Serve immediately.

🌑 JUICY TIP
Red raspberries are high in vitamin C and are a powerhouse of antioxidants. Add these little rubies to your juice drinks to help boost immunity and slow down the effects of aging.

Grapefruit Apple Soda

Makes 12 to 16 ounces (355 to 475 ml)

If you like grapefruit but aren't always a fan of the strong sourness, this sweet fizzy drink is for you. The apple balances out the bitterness and won't make you pucker.

1 grapefruit
1 apple
½ cup (120 ml) cold sparkling water

1. Cut the peel off of the grapefruit and slice it into wedges. Core the apple and cut it into slices.

2. Juice the grapefruit and apple together.

3. Pour the juice into a large glass and add the sparkling water. Serve immediately.

◀ Watermelon Soda

Makes 12 to 16 ounces (355 to 475 ml)

Watermelon makes a lively pink-hued juice soda. You'll love this for a girls' get-together.

2 cups (300 g) watermelon chunks
½ cup (120 ml) cold sparkling water

1. Juice the watermelon.

2. Pour the juice into a large glass and add the sparkling water. Serve immediately.

Blackberry Apple Soda

Makes 12 to 16 ounces (355 to 475 ml)

This flavorful drink reminds me of blackberry pie, but in a fizzy juice!

> 1 apple
> 2 cups (290 g) blackberries
> ½ cup (120 ml) cold sparkling water

1. Core the apple and cut it into slices.

2. Juice the apple and blackberries together, alternating the two kinds of produce as you juice (see page 23).

3. Pour the juice into a large glass and add the sparkling water. Serve immediately.

Spicy Pear Soda

Makes 12 to 16 ounces (355 to 475 ml)

The ginger and cucumber enhance the flavor of the pear in this spicy drink.

> 1 pear
> 2-inch (5 cm) piece of cucumber
> 1-inch (2.5 cm) piece of fresh ginger
> ½ cup (120 ml) cold sparkling water

1. Core the pear and cut it into slices.

2. Juice the pear, cucumber, and ginger together, alternating the different kinds of produce as you juice (see page 23).

3. Pour the juice into a large glass and add the sparkling water. Serve immediately.

☞ **JUICY TIP**
Adding ginger to your fruit sodas will give them a "ginger ale" feel. Feel free to experiment with more than a 1-inch (2.5 cm) length, if you enjoy the flavor.

BLENDER
JUICES

For those days when you just want the convenience of using your blender and do not want to juice in your juicer, blender juices are your new best friends. These blended juices are different from smoothies because they are not as thick and can pass for real juice. Bonus: They are typically quicker than juicing and you'll need less produce because you'll be including the fiber. Bottoms up!

Pineapple Nectar

Makes 12 to 16 ounces (355 to 475 ml)

Sweet pineapple blends beautifully with orange to create a perfect breakfast juice.

> 1 orange
> 1 cup (165 g) fresh pineapple chunks
> ½ cup (120 ml) cold water

1. Cut the peel off of the orange and slice it into wedges.

2. Put the orange, pineapple, and water in your blender. Blend on high speed until smooth. Add more water, if you like. Serve immediately.

☞ **JUICY TIP**

Don't be afraid of fruit-heavy blended juices. Consuming blended fruit juices is ideal for those with blood sugar issues. When you blend your juice, the fiber is consumed with the juice, allowing your body to digest the fruit sugars more slowly.

Grape Lucky ▶

Makes 12 to 16 ounces (355 to 475 ml)

Lemon balances out the sweetness of the grapes in this tangy version of grape juice.

> 1 lemon
> 2 cups (300 g) grapes
> ½ cup (120 ml) cold water

1. Cut the peel off of the lemon and slice it into wedges.

2. Put the lemon and grapes in your blender. Blend on high speed until smooth. Add more water, if you like. Serve immediately.

Watermelon Sling

Makes 12 to 16 ounces (355 to 475 ml)

Nothing is more refreshing than a watermelon and lime combo.

> 1 lime
> 1½ cups (225 g) watermelon chunks

1. Cut the peel off of the lime and slice it into wedges.

2. Put the lime and the watermelon in your blender. Blend on high speed until smooth. Add cold water, if you like. Serve immediately.

⚠ JUICY TIP

Melons and citrus fruits are very juicy and blend easily. Dense fruits like apples will need more liquid to process. If you prefer thinner juices, add more water to your blender.

Peachy Cider

Makes 12 to 16 ounces (355 to 475 ml)

I love the sweet, sinful taste of this antioxidant-packed blend.

> 2 peaches
> 1 cup (150 g) grapes
> 1 cup (235 ml) cold water

1. Pit the peaches and cut them into slices.

2. Put the peaches, grapes, and water in your blender. Blend on high speed until smooth. Add more water, if you like. Serve immediately.

Grapefruit Sun

Makes 12 to 16 ounces (355 to 475 ml)

Are you in love with grapefruit? This minty lime version is something you'd never imagine would taste so good.

> 1 grapefruit
> 1 lime
> 2 sprigs of fresh mint
> ½ cup (120 ml) cold water

1. Cut the peel off of the grapefruit and slice it into wedges. Cut the peel off of the lime and cut it in half.

2. Put the grapefruit, lime, mint, and water in your blender. Blend on high speed until smooth. Add more water, if you like. Serve immediately.

Tropical Craze

Makes 12 to 16 ounces (355 to 475 ml)

Quench your thirst with this sweet favorite from the islands.

1 mango
1 kiwifruit
1 cup (165 g) fresh pineapple chunks
½ cup (120 ml) cold water

1. Cut the peel off of the mango and discard the pit. Cut the flesh into spears or chunks. Peel the kiwi and cut it into wedges.

2. Put the mango, kiwi, pineapple, and water in your blender. Blend on high speed until smooth. Add more water, if you like. Serve immediately.

> ☞ **JUICY TIP**
> Unlike juicing in a juicer, using frozen fruit in blended juices is fine, but you'll have to add additional water to allow the blender to process smoothly.

Apple Slumber

Makes 12 to 16 ounces (355 to 475 ml)

If you need a quick detox drink to recover from a few days of heavy eating, this juice will nourish your whole system.

2 apples
1 lemon
1 kale leaf
1 cup (235 ml) cold water

1. Core the apples and cut them into slices. Remove the peel from the lemon and slice it into wedges. Remove the stem from the kale and chop the leaf.

2. Put the apples, lemon, kale, and water in your blender. Blend on high speed until smooth. Add more water, if you like. Serve immediately.

◀ Green Heaven

Makes 12 to 16 ounces (355 to 475 ml)

This amazing peach-spinach combo is a perfect way to get your greens in.

> 2 peaches
> ½ of a pear
> ½ cup (15 g) spinach leaves
> 1 cup (235 ml) cold water

1. Pit the peaches and cut them into slices. Core the pear half and cut it into slices.

2. Put the peaches, pear, spinach, and water in your blender. Blend on high speed until smooth. Add more water, if you like. Serve immediately.

Lemon Buzz

Makes 12 to 16 ounces (355 to 475 ml)

Make this sour pineapple-based juice for a midafternoon treat.

> 1 lemon
> 1 cup (165 g) fresh pineapple chunks
> ½ cup (120 ml) cold water

1. Cut the peel off of the lemon and slice it into wedges.

2. Put the lemon, pineapple, and water in your blender. Blend on high speed until smooth. Add more water, if you like. Serve immediately.

Mango Fix

Makes 12 to 16 ounces (355 to 475 ml)

This cleansing drink is the ultimate refresher and a great way to benefit from the many nutrients in parsley.

> 2 mangoes
> 1 bunch of fresh parsley
> 1 cup (235 ml) cold water

1. Cut the peel off of the mangoes and discard the pits. Cut the flesh into spears or chunks.

2. Put the mangoes, parsley, and water in your blender. Blend on high speed until smooth. Add more water, if you like. Serve immediately.

Red Grape Rambler

Makes 12 to 16 ounces (355 to 475 ml)

I love this juice in the morning when I'm tight on time. It's nourishing and cleansing, and it gets you moving.

> 1 medium orange
> 1 banana
> 1 cup (150 g) red grapes
> ½ cup (120 ml) cold water

1. Cut the peel off of the orange and slice it into wedges. Remove the peel from the banana and cut it into slices.

2. Put the orange, banana, grapes, and water in your blender. Blend on high speed until smooth. Add more water, if you like. Serve immediately.

Green Melon Glow

Makes 12 to 16 ounces (355 to 475 ml)

This quick and easy watermelon juice will hydrate you from the inside out.

> 2 cups (300 g) watermelon chunks
> 2 romaine lettuce leaves
> ½ cup (120 ml) cold water

1. Put the watermelon, romaine lettuce, and water in your blender.

2. Blend on high speed until smooth. Add more water, if you like. Serve immediately.

Pear Delight

Makes 12 to 16 ounces (355 to 475 ml)

Sweet pear and mint are a combination made in heaven.

> 2 pears
> 2 kale leaves
> 1 small bunch of fresh mint
> 1 cup (235 ml) cold water

1. Core the pears and cut them into slices. Remove the stems from the kale and chop the leaves.

2. Put the pears, kale, mint, and water in your blender. Blend on high speed until smooth. Add more water, if you like. Serve immediately.

◀ Kiwi-tini

Makes 12 to 16 ounces (355 to 475 ml)

Kiwifruits make amazing blended juices. You'll love this tasty, unexpected pairing with celery and banana.

2 kiwifruits
1 banana
1 celery stalk
1 cup (235 ml) cold water

1. Peel the kiwis and slice them into wedges. Peel the banana and cut it into slices. Cut the celery into ½-inch (1.3 cm) pieces.

2. Put the kiwis, banana, celery, and water in your blender. Blend on high speed until smooth. Add more water, if you like. Serve immediately.

Strawberry Twist

Makes 12 to 16 ounces (355 to 475 ml)

If you've got strawberries and mangoes, don't pass up this dessert-like combination.

> 1 mango
> 10 strawberries
> 1 cup (235 ml) cold water

1. Cut the peel off of the mango and discard the pit. Cut the flesh into spears or chunks.

2. Put the mango, strawberries, and water in your blender. Blend on high speed until smooth. Add more water, if you like. Serve immediately.

Green Sipper

Makes 12 to 16 ounces (355 to 475 ml)

Sneak the spinach into this refreshing apple and lime combination. You might find it relieves constipation, too.

> 2 apples
> 1 lime
> 1 cup (30 g) spinach leaves
> 1 cup (235 ml) cold water

1. Core the apples and cut them into slices. Cut the peel off of the lime and cut it in half.

2. Put the apples, lime, spinach, and water in your blender. Blend on high speed until smooth. Add more water, if you like. Serve immediately.

Apricot Reviver ▶

Makes 12 to 16 ounces (355 to 475 ml)

Take advantage of the apricot harvest when the fruits are at their ripest! This is the ultimate summertime drink. Add ¼ cup (38 g) of blueberries for an extra boost.

> 2 apricots
> 1 banana
> ½ cup (235 ml) cold water

1. Pit the apricots and cut them into slices. Remove the peel from the banana and cut it into slices.

2. Put the apricots, banana, and water in your blender. Blend on high speed until smooth. Add more water, if you like. Serve immediately.

Carrot Papaya Punch ▶

Makes 12 to 16 ounces (355 to 475 ml)

Papaya isn't ideal for juicing in a juicer, but it's absolutely perfect in blended juices and mixes fabulously with carrot.

> 2 carrots
> 1 cup (140 g) papaya chunks
> 1 cup (235 ml) cold water

1. Cut the carrots into ½-inch (1.3 cm) pieces.

2. Put the carrots, papaya, and water in your blender. Blend on high speed until smooth. Add more water, if you like. Serve immediately.

Honeydew Quencher

Makes 12 to 16 ounces (355 to 475 ml)

Perfect on a Friday night to wind down from a hectic and busy week, this juice tastes like a party cocktail.

> 1 lime
> 2 cups (340 g) honeydew chunks
> 1 cup (235 ml) cold water

1. Remove the peel from the lime and cut it in half.

2. Put the lime, honeydew, and water in your blender. Blend on high speed until smooth. Add more water, if you like. Serve immediately.

☞**JUICY TIP**
If you like sweeter blended juices, add 1 or 2 pitted dates or 1 tablespoon (20 g) of honey to your blend.

Raspberry Pear Punch

Makes 12 to 16 ounces (355 to 475 ml)

This mildly sweet blend is a great choice at breakfast time.

> 2 pears
> ½ of a lime
> ½ cup (65 g) raspberries
> 1 cup (235 ml) cold water

1. Core the pears and cut them into slices. Cut the peel off the lime half.

2. Put the pears, lime, raspberries, and water in your blender. Blend on high speed until smooth. Add more water, if you like. Serve immediately.

💧 **JUICY TIP**
Do you want a creamy blended juice that will keep you fuller longer? Add ¼ of an avocado to your blend.

Carrot Apple Warmer

Makes 12 to 16 ounces (355 to 475 ml)

Grab the blanket and a movie and spice up your winter night with this sweet ginger drink!

> 1 carrot
> 1 apple
> 1 small slice of fresh ginger
> 1 cup (235 ml) cold water

1. Cut the carrot into ½-inch (1.3 cm) pieces. Core the apple and cut it into slices.

2. Put the carrot, apple, ginger, and water in your blender. Blend on high speed until smooth. Add more water, if you like. Serve immediately.

Grapefruit Getaway

Makes 12 to 16 ounces (355 to 475 ml)

I always love grapefruit in a weekend breakfast juice. You can make this one quickly and easily if you're tight on time.

> 1 orange
> 1 grapefruit
> ½ cup (120 ml) coconut water

1. Cut the peel off of the orange and slice it into wedges. Cut the peel off of the grapefruit and slice it into wedges.

2. Put the orange, grapefruit, and coconut water in your blender. Blend on high speed until smooth. Add more coconut water, if you like. Serve immediately.

🥥 **JUICY TIP**

Coconut water can always be substituted for water in your blended juice.

◀ Pink Goddess

Makes 12 to 16 ounces (355 to 475 ml)

Combine the powerful antioxidants in berries and the vitamins in honeydew melon and you'll be glowing in no time.

> 5 strawberries
> 1 cup (170 g) honeydew chunks
> ¼ cup (33 g) raspberries
> ½ cup (120 ml) cold water

1. Put the strawberries, honeydew, raspberries, and water in your blender. Blend on high speed until smooth. Add more water, if you like. Serve immediately.

☞ **JUICY TIP**
To turn your blended juice into a creamy smoothie, add nut milk or coconut milk instead of water to your drink before blending.

◄ Orange Swinger

Makes 12 to 16 ounces (355 to 475 ml)

If you like tangy or sour flavors, this vitamin C–packed drink will be right up your alley.

 2 oranges
 1 small lemon
 ½ cup (120 ml) cold water

1. Cut the peels off of the oranges and slice them into wedges. Cut the peel off of the lemon and slice it into wedges.

2. Put the oranges, lemon, and water in your blender. Blend on high speed until smooth. Add more water, if you like. Serve immediately.

Carrot Orange Swirl

Makes 12 to 16 ounces (355 to 475 ml)

Pineapple contains bromelain, which may help with natural pain relief. The carrot and orange add high doses of vitamins A and C, making this one healthful drink. Replace the water with coconut milk to turn this juice into a creamy tropical drink.

 1 carrot
 1 orange
 1 cup (165 g) fresh pineapple chunks
 ½ cup (120 ml) cold water

1. Cut the carrot into ½-inch (1.3 cm) pieces. Cut the peel off of the orange and slice it into wedges.

2. Put the carrot, orange, pineapple, and water in your blender. Blend on high speed until smooth. Add more water, if you like. Serve immediately.

Cucumber Spiral

Makes 12 to 16 ounces (355 to 475 ml)

This flavorful, sweet juice is a great option to help reduce belly bloat.

> 2 peaches
> ½ of a cucumber
> 4 strawberries
> 1 cup (235 ml) cold water

1. Pit the peaches and cut them into slices. Cut the cucumber into small slices.

2. Put the peaches, cucumber, strawberries, and water in your blender. Blend on high speed until smooth. Add more water if you like. Serve immediately.

Melon Rosa

Makes 12 to 16 ounces (355 to 475 ml)

Do you love watermelon? You'll really want to try this fruity and tangy mix.

> 1 lemon
> 1 orange
> 1 cup (150 g) watermelon chunks
> ½ cup (120 ml) cold water

1. Cut the peel off of the lemon and cut it in half. Cut the peel off of the orange and slice it into wedges.

2. Put the lemon, orange, watermelon, and water in your blender. Blend on high speed until smooth. Add more water, if you like. Serve immediately.

☞ **JUICY TIP**
If you like a cooler, thicker juice, add ice to your mixture before you blend it.

◀ Sweet Flamingo

Makes 12 to 16 ounces (355 to 475 ml)

This spicy, sweet blend is just what the doctor ordered for better digestion.

1 orange
1 cup (140 g) papaya chunks
1 small slice of fresh ginger or
   ½ teaspoon ground ginger
½ cup (120 ml) cold water

1. Cut the peel off of the orange and slice it into wedges.

2. Place the orange, papaya, ginger, and water in your blender. Blend on high speed until smooth. Add more water, if you like. Serve immediately.

☞ **JUICY TIP**
Adding ground spices like ginger or turmeric or wheatgrass powder is an easy way to enhance the nutritional value of your blended juice.

Pineapple Peach Party

Makes 12 to 16 ounces (355 to 475 ml)

Do you need a midday pick-me-up? This green blend will do the trick.

    1 peach
    1 cup (165 g) fresh pineapple chunks
    ½ cup (15 g) spinach leaves
    1 cup (235 ml) cold water

1. Pit the peach and cut it into slices.

2. Put the peach, pineapple, spinach, and water in your blender. Blend on high speed until smooth. Add more water, if you like. Serve immediately.

Melon Hurricane ▶

Makes 12 to 16 ounces (355 to 475 ml)

Celebrate a warm summer night with sweet melons. This juice is great over ice.

    1 cup (150 g) watermelon chunks
    1 cup (160 g) cantaloupe chunks
    ½ cup (120 ml) cold water

1. Put the watermelon, cantaloupe, and water in your blender. Blend on high speed until smooth. Add more water, if you like. Serve immediately.

Tomato Dream ▶

Makes 12 to 16 ounces (355 to 475 ml)

Even if you aren't a tomato fan, you'll love it in this juice.

> 1 orange
> 1 mango
> ½ of a tomato
> ½ cup (120 ml) cold water

1. Cut the peel off of the orange and cut it into wedges. Cut the peel off of the mango and discard the pit. Cut the flesh into spears or chunks. Slice the tomato half into wedges.

2. Put the orange, mango, tomato, and water into your blender. Blend on high speed until smooth. Add more water, if you like. Serve immediately.

Red Cardinal

Makes 12 to 16 ounces (355 to 475 ml)

This savory juice can be made saltier with the addition of more celery.

> 2 carrots
> 1 celery stalk
> 1 tomato
> ½ cup (120 ml) cold water

1. Cut the carrots and celery into ½-inch (1.3 cm) pieces. Slice the tomato into wedges.

2. Put the carrots, celery, tomato, and water in your blender. Blend on high speed until smooth. Add more water, if you like. Serve immediately.

⬤ JUICY TIP
Try making juice and then mixing it with whole fruit, like bananas or avocados, in your blender to gain the benefits of both juicing and smoothies in one drink.

Cucumber Apple Fancy

Makes 12 to 16 ounces (355 to 475 ml)

Cucumber can help regulate body temperature. Hydrate on a hot summer day or after a workout with this extremely refreshing cooler.

> 1 apple
> 1 cucumber
> ½ of a lime
> 1 cup (235 ml) cold water

1. Core the apple and cut it into slices. Cut the cucumber into small slices. Cut the peel off of the lime.

2. Put the apple, cucumber, lime, and water in your blender. Blend on high speed until smooth. Add more water, if you like. Serve immediately.

◀ Cranberry Kiss

Makes 12 to 16 ounces (355 to 475 ml)

This tart and sweet combination will knock your socks off.

> 1 cup (150 g) grapes
> ¼ cup (25 g) cranberries
> ½ cup (75 g) watermelon chunks
> ½ cup (120 ml) cold water

1. Put the grapes, cranberries, watermelon, and water in your blender. Blend on high speed until smooth. Add more water, if you like. Serve immediately.

Apple Tango

Makes 12 to 16 ounces (355 to 475 ml)

Banana makes this dreamy apple blend another good option for breakfast or to keep you full until your next meal.

> 1 apple
> 1 celery stalk
> 1 banana
> ½ of a cucumber
> ½ cup (120 ml) cold water

1. Core the apple and cut it into slices. Cut the celery into ½-inch (1.3 cm) pieces. Peel the banana and cut it into slices. Cut the cucumber half into small slices.

2. Put the apple, celery, banana, cucumber, and water in your blender. Blend on high speed until smooth. Add more water, if you like. Serve immediately.

☞ JUICY TIP

Blended juice tastes best when consumed immediately but will typically store longer than juice made in a juicer. If you want to store your blender juice, seal it in an airtight glass container in the refrigerator for up to 12 hours. Storing it longer will affect the taste.

Green Ginger-ade

Makes 12 to 16 ounces (355 to 475 ml)

Spicy and refreshing, this detoxifying combination is perfect for breakfast. For digestive issues, add a splash of aloe juice.

½ of a cucumber, chopped
1 lemon, peeled
1 small slice of fresh ginger
7 mint leaves
1 cup (30 g) spinach
1 apple, cored and chopped
½ cup (120 ml) cold coconut water

1. Put the cucumber, lemon, ginger, mint, spinach, apple, and coconut water into your blender. Blend on high speed until smooth. Serve immediately.

Lemon-berry Sunburst

Makes 12 to 16 ounces (355 to 475 ml)

You'll come back to this low-sugar and delightfully sour drink over and over again.

1 cup (125 g) raspberries
1 pear, cored and chopped
1 lemon, peeled
1 cup (235 ml) cold water

1. Add the raspberries, pear, lemon, and water to your blender. Blend on high speed until smooth. Serve immediately.

Spicy Carrot Tonic

Makes 12 to 16 ounces (355 to 475 ml)

This anti-inflammatory blend is sweet and satisfying. Try using full fat coconut milk and crushed ice instead of water to make this into a creamy treat.

1 apple, cored and chopped
1 carrot, chopped
½ cup (83 g) pineapple chunks
1 small slice of fresh ginger
1 small slice of fresh turmeric
1 cup (235 ml) cold water

1. Add the apple, carrot, pineapple, ginger, turmeric, and water to your blender. Blend on high speed until smooth. Serve immediately.

☞ **JUICY TIP**
Room temperature drinks are better for digestion, but blended juices often taste better served over ice or blended with crushed ice. Experiment with ice in your blended drinks to see what you prefer.

ACKNOWLEDGMENTS

This book and everything that led up to its creation have been inspired and supported by many amazing people. I'm humbled and grateful to be the one to share how fabulous juicing is through this medium.

Writing a juicing book is no easy task, but having an incredible, passionate team behind you makes the process much easier. A heartfelt thank-you to everyone at Harvard Common Press and Quarto Publishing, including my brilliant editor, Dan Rosenberg.

To Adam, thanks for always taste-testing my juice creations, cleaning up the juicer, and supporting me each step of the way. You couldn't be a better partner, and I'm eternally thankful for you.

Hugs to my amazing family: Mom, Dad, Derek, Anne, and all the Simkins, for supporting and encouraging me. I feel very blessed to be a part of your lives.

And for all my prayers answered and big dreams that have come to pass, my biggest love and gratitude goes to God.

Most important, thank you to my readers! I'm overjoyed that my book has made it into your hands and my juices into your cup.

ABOUT THE AUTHOR

Vanessa Simkins is the creator and writer of the website and newsletter All About Juicing (AllAboutJuicing.com), which serves up fresh, tested juices and juicing advice for optimal flavor and health.

A juicing trendsetter known for her inventive and tasty juice recipes, Vanessa has an undying thirst for connecting people back to what makes them healthy, one drink at a time. She lives in Austin, Texas, with her husband, Adam, and cat, Rio.

INDEX

almond milk
  Apricot Almond Milk
    Juice, 202
  Blueberry Almond Milk
    Juice, 195
  Carrot Almond Milk
    Juice, 195
  Raspberry Almond Milk
    Juice, 198
  Strawberry Almond Milk
    Juice, 201
aloe
  Aloe Vera Apple Shot, 273
  introduction to, 17
apples
  ABC Juice, 213
  Aloe Vera Apple Shot, 273
  Apple Cinnamon Pecan
    Milk Juice, 210
  Apple Flip, 112
  Apple, Mint, and Chia
    Juice, 190
  Apple, Orange, and Chia
    Juice, 182
  Apple Pomegranate
    Soda, 299
  Apple Slumber, 319
  Apple Tango, 339
  Awesome Apple, 218
  Bashful Blueberry, 223
  Basil Buzz, 73
  Basil Strawberry
    Lemonade, 161
  Beach Babe Bomber, 147
  Beet-ade, 62
  Beet Slinger, 38
  Berry Fix, 114
  Blackberry Apple Soda, 314
  Blackberry Bliss, 113
  Blackberry Mint
    Lemonade, 168
  Blueberry Lemonade, 158

Bodacious Berry, 222
Broccoli Breeze, 63
Caipirinha Crush, 145
Carrot Apple Warmer, 328
Carrot, Apricot, and Chia
  Juice, 189
Carrot Crush, 31
Carrot Lemonade, 175
Carrot Rosemary
  Cocktail, 80
Chard Angel, 61
Cherry Lemonade, 171
Cherry Power, 65
Cilantro Crush, 75
Citrus Breakfast, 127
Citrus Crush, 53
Constipation Reliever, 251
Cranberry, Apple, and Grape
  Soda, 302
Cranberry, Apple, and Lime
  Punch, 293
Cranberry, Apple, Grape,
  and Chia Juice, 180
Cranberry Apple
  Smash, 102
Cranberry Vitality, 253
Crazy Cranberry Apple, 223
Cucumber Apple Fancy, 337
Cucumber Dawn, 59
Cucumber, Kale, and Chia
  Juice, 181
Daytime Detox, 253
Detox Shot, 275
Dill Angel, 85
Dinosaur Power, 219
Energy Cocktail, 33
Energy Elixir, 239
Flaming Fennel, 39
Garden Glow, 46
Gentle Detox Sipper, 256
Ginger Hot Spot, 60
Ginger Lemonade, 167

Ginger Mixer, 37
Golden Sunset, 47
Grape Apple Soda, 305
Grapefruit Apple Soda, 312
Grapefruit, Beet, Apple, and
  Chia Juice, 185
Grapefruit Lemonade, 169
Grapefruit Sunrise, 119
Green Apple Twist, 68
Green Cider, 54
Green Craze, 70
Green Detoxer, 263
Green Ginger-ade, 340
Green Glory, 48
Green Goddess, 52
Green Grape Soda, 311
Green Jolt, 230
Green Julep, 81
Green Lemonade, 172
Green Limeade, 66
Green Power Punch, 218
Green Sipper, 324
Green Slammer, 69
Green Stimulant, 235
Green Swizzle, 51
Herb Heaven, 93
Herby Green Cleanser, 250
introduction to, 23–24
Jalapeño Lemonade, 174
Jamaica Kiss, 147
Kale Aces, 54
Kale Apple Shot, 280
Kale Quencher, 56
Key Lime Cocktail, 120
Kiwi Divine, 156
Kiwi Lemonade, 172
Kiwi Smash, 70
Lemon, Apple, and Beet
  Punch, 284
Lemon Lime Ale, 123
Lemon Meringue, 138
Lime Mint Lemonade, 175

Lime Zing, 239
Lovely Lemon, 220
Melon Balancer, 254
Midday Calmer, 244
Mint-ade, 51
Morning Magic, 236
Orange Lemonade, 160
Orange Vitality, 232
Oregano Royale, 87
Parsley Power, 233
Parsnip Parfait, 45
Peaceful Breeze, 245
Peach Lemonade, 169
Pear Apple Soda, 301
Pear Plush, 96
Persimmon Twist, 107
Pineapple Dawn, 40
Pineapple Lemonade, 174
Pink Parfait, 110
Pomegranate Cider, 105
Popeye Punch, 215
Radically Red Berry, 219
Radical Radish, 216
Raspberry, Apple, and Chia
  Juice, 190
Raspberry Lemonade, 161
Raspberry Lemon Soda, 307
Raspberry Mint Lemonade,
  163
Raspberry Rambler, 99
Red Beet Lemonade, 171
Red Beet, Orange, and
  Apple Punch, 288
Red Cabbage Apple
  Shot, 278
Red Rainbow Juice, 213
Red Reviver, 57
Red Warrior, 47
Relax-tini, 244
Rosemary Grapefruit
  Guzzler, 92
Rosemary Lemonade, 166

Rosemary Slammer, 83
Rose Punch, 97
Rose Royale, 129
Ruby Slumber, 46
Scarlet Sizzle, 115
seeds, 21
Skinny Apple Cleanser, 264
Skinny Sipper, 260
Sleepy Punch, 242
Slender Swizzle, 262
Slimming Tonic, 259
Sour Apple Soda, 301
Spearmint Sour, 90
Spicy Apple Ginger
    Soda, 307
Spicy Carrot Tonic, 340
Spicy Orange Sunrise, 125
Spirulina Apple Shot, 273
Strawberry Basil Blush, 73
Strawberry Lemonade, 163
Super Celery Cooler, 215
Super Greens Shot, 269
Super Slimmer, 266
Sweet Lemonade, 159
Sweet Lime Lemonade, 164
Sweet Orange Soda, 300
Tangerine Peach Lemonade,
    164
Tarragon Lemon-ale, 86
Tart Apple Soda, 305
Thyme Toddy, 78
Triple Power, 230
Veggie Starlet, 32
Wacky Strawberry, 222
Watermelon Lemonade, 168
Watermelon Strawberry
    Lemonade, 166
Wellness Shot, 280
Zucchini Zing, 63
apricots
    Apricot Almond Milk
        Juice, 202
    Apricot Angel, 104
    Apricot Reviver, 324
    Carrot, Apricot, and Chia
        Juice, 189
    Pineapple Apricot Pecan
        Milk Juice, 208
    Soothing Swizzle, 246
arugula
    Cherry Power, 65
    Jade Oasis, 59
    Mango Fusion, 69

avocados
    introduction to, 17
    Raspberry Pear Punch, 327

bananas
    Apple Tango, 339
    Apricot Reviver, 324
    Kiwi-tini, 323
    Red Grape Rambler, 322
basil
    Basil Buzz, 73
    Basil Strawberry Lemonade,
        161
    Golden Breeze, 148
    Strawberry Basil Blush, 73
beets
    ABC Juice, 213
    Beet-ade, 62
    Beet Slinger, 38
    Beet Sunrise, 34
    Citrus Fusion, 126
    Detox Shot, 275
    Flaming Fennel, 39
    Grapefruit, Beet, Apple, and
        Chia Juice, 185
    Hawaiian Sun, 156
    introduction to, 24
    Lemon, Apple, and Beet
        Punch, 284
    Liver Elixir, 254
    Metabolism Booster, 267
    Orange, Beet, and Chia
        Juice, 192
    Oregano Oasis, 76
    Pink Sunburst, 126
    Red Beet Ginger Shot, 270
    Red Beet Lemonade, 171
    Red Beet Lemon Shot, 273
    Red Beet, Orange, and
        Apple Punch, 288
    Red Rainbow Juice, 213
    Red Reviver, 57
    Red Warrior, 47
    Red Zing, 233
    Rosemary Slammer, 83
    Ruby Slumber, 46
    Scarlet Sizzle, 115
    Sweet Thyme Rosemary
        Punch, 89
    V6 Juice, 40
    Veggie Starlet, 32
bell peppers
    Carrot Pep-Up, 233

Cayenne Kicker, 34
Clementine Daisy, 132
introduction to, 24
Oregano Royale, 87
Red Cadillac, 48
Red Pepper Plush, 40
Skinny Sipper, 260
Tomato Trim-Down, 264
Veg Crush, 39
Yellow Sling, 97
blackberries
    Berry Slammer, 130
    Blackberry Apple Soda, 314
    Blackberry Bliss, 113
    Blackberry Mint Lemonade,
        168
    Blackberry, Pear, and Chia
        Juice, 189
    Blackberry Pineapple
        Punch, 293
    Blackberry Vanilla Cashew
        Milk Juice, 204
    Blood Orange Cocktail, 122
blood oranges
    Blood Orange Cocktail, 122
    Flaming Orange, 139
blueberries
    Apricot Reviver, 324
    Bashful Blueberry, 223
    Blueberry Almond Milk
        Juice, 195
    Blueberry, Grape, and Chia
        Juice, 186
    Blueberry Grape Soda, 304
    Blueberry Lemonade, 158
    Blueberry Macadamia Milk
        Juice, 204
    Blueberry Sparkle, 114
    Bodacious Berry, 222
    Grape Oasis, 108
    Mixed-Berry Pistachio Milk
        Juice, 197
    Orangeberry Oasis, 137
    Stress-Free Cocktail, 241
broccoli
    Broccoli Balancer, 53
    Broccoli Breeze, 63
    Garden Glow, 46
    Green Craze, 70
    Green Jolt, 230
    Green Monster, 222
    Green Power Punch, 218
    introduction to, 24

Pear Temptation, 152
Veg Crush, 39
cabbage
    Carrot Kick, 256
    Detox Shot, 275
    Ginger Hot Spot, 60
    introduction to, 24
    Purple Cocktail, 113
    Purple Daisy, 48
    Red Cabbage Apple
        Shot, 278
    Sage Booster, 88
cantaloupe
    Bermuda Rose, 150
    Cantaloupe Blush, 101
    Cantaloupe Fat Buster, 267
    Magical Melon, 218
    Melon Hurricane, 334
    Melon Twist, 138
    Melon Zingo, 108
    Pink Melon-ade, 96
    Ruby Melone, 147
    Sunny Swizzle, 154
carrot greens, avoiding, 22
carrots
    Acne Fix, 251
    All-Star Favorite, 216
    Apple Flip, 112
    Asparagus Ace, 37
    Bahia Cocktail, 150
    Beet Slinger, 38
    Beet Sunrise, 34
    Broccoli Breeze, 63
    Cantaloupe Fat Buster, 267
    Carrot Almond Milk
        Juice, 195
    Carrot Apple Warmer, 328
    Carrot, Apricot, and Chia
        Juice, 189
    Carrot Cashew Milk
        Juice, 207
    Carrot Crush, 31
    Carrot Dandy, 42
    Carrot Kick, 256
    Carrot Lemonade, 175
    Carrot, Lemon, and
        Pineapple Punch, 289
    Carrot Mango Cashew Milk
        Juice, 209
    Carrot, Orange, and Chia
        Juice, 186
    Carrot Orange Swirl, 331
    Carrot Papaya Punch, 326

Carrot Pep-Up, 233
Carrot, Pineapple, and Chia
    Juice, 182
Carrot Rosemary Cocktail,
    80
Celery Reviver, 249
Cilantro Crush, 75
Cold and Flu Shot, 271
Dill Daisy, 89
Emerald Energizer, 57
Energy Cocktail, 33
Energy Elixir, 239
Fruity Parsley Punch, 79
Garden Glow, 46
Ginger Mixer, 37
Golden Sunset, 47
Green Jolt, 230
Green Stimulant, 235
Herb Heaven, 93
introduction to, 24
Kale Aces, 54
Lean Beauty Punch, 263
Lemon Alkalizer, 259
Liver Elixir, 254
Mango Viva, 154
Metabolism Booster, 267
Orange Slumber, 117
Oregano Oasis, 76
Parsnip Parfait, 45
Pineapple Dawn, 40
Pineapple Hot Stuff, 260
Pineapple, Mango, and
    Carrot Punch, 288
Purple Daisy, 48
Radical Radish, 216
Raspberry Rambler, 99
Red Cadillac, 48
Red Cardinal, 337
Red Pepper Plush, 40
Red Warrior, 47
Red Zing, 233
Sage Sunrise, 76
Scarlet Night, 46
Soothing Swizzle, 246
Spicy Carrot Tonic, 340
Sweet Potato Buzz, 235
Sweet Potato Sunshine, 37
Sweet Sunrise, 66
Tarragon Cocktail, 83
Thyme Pineapple Juice, 93
Tranquil Toddy, 245
V6 Juice, 40
Veg Crush, 39

Veggie Starlet, 32
Veggie-tini, 42
Veg Royale, 31
Wheatgrass Reviver, 232
Yummy Carrot Craze, 225
cashew milk
    Blackberry Vanilla Cashew
        Milk Juice, 204
    Carrot Cashew Milk
        Juice, 207
    Carrot Mango Cashew Milk
        Juice, 209
    Chocolate Strawberry
        Cashew Milk Juice, 203
    Peach Cinnamon Cashew
        Milk Juice, 199
    Pineapple Cashew Milk
        Juice, 198
    Strawberry Mango Cashew
        Milk Juice, 200
cauliflower, in Carrot
    Dandy, 42
cayenne pepper
    Cayenne Kicker, 34
    Ginger, Lemon, and
        Cayenne Shot, 277
    Immune Booster Shot, 281
    introduction to, 17
    Pineapple Hot Stuff, 260
    Red Pepper Plush, 40
celery
    ABC Juice, 213
    Apple Tango, 339
    Asparagus Ace, 37
    Bedtime Flip, 242
    Bodacious Berry, 222
    Broccoli Balancer, 53
    Carrot Kick, 256
    Cayenne Kicker, 34
    Celery Reviver, 249
    Cilantro Celery Punch, 86
    Crazy Cranberry Apple, 223
    Emerald Energizer, 57
    Fantastic Pear Punch, 226
    Garden Glow, 46
    Golden Sunset, 47
    Grape, Lemon, and Chia
        Juice, 178
    Grape Oasis, 108
    Green Apple Twist, 68
    Green Cider, 54
    Green Daisy, 62
    Green Detoxer, 263

Green Glory, 48
Green Goddess, 52
Green Grape Celery
    Punch, 292
Green Grape Soda, 311
Green Julep, 81
Green Limeade, 66
Green Remedy, 65
Green Stimulant, 235
Green Swizzle, 51
Herby Green Cleanser, 250
introduction to, 24
juicing tips, 22
Kale Quencher, 56
Kiwi Divine, 156
Kiwi Mint-ade, 79
Kiwi Smash, 70
Kiwi-tini, 323
Lean Beauty Punch, 263
Mango Fusion, 69
Metabolism Booster, 267
Mint Melody, 75
Orange Zing, 33
Oregano Royale, 87
Peach-tastic, 102
Pineapple Dawn, 40
Pineapple Spearmint
    Cooler, 92
Red Cardinal, 337
Red Warrior, 47
Relax-tini, 244
Rosemary Slammer, 83
Ruby Slumber, 46
Sage Booster, 88
Scarlet Night, 46
Skinny Apple Cleanser, 264
Skinny Mini Cocktail, 258
Slender Swizzle, 262
Slumber Elixir, 246
Soothing Swizzle, 246
Spearmint Sour, 90
Spicy Apple Ginger
    Soda, 307
Spicy Pear Slim-Down, 267
Super Celery Cooler, 215
Super Slimmer, 266
Tension Tamer Tonic, 241
Thyme Toddy, 78
Tomato Tonic, 43
V6 Juice, 40
Veggie Starlet, 32
Veggie Tonic, 45
Veg Royale, 31

Wellness Shot, 280
Wheatgrass Reviver, 232
chard
    Chard Angel, 61
    Chard Booster, 60
    introduction to, 27
    Midday Calmer, 244
cherries
    Brazilian Glow, 150
    Cheerful Cherry, 220
    Cherry Craze, 104
    Cherry Lemonade, 171
    Cherry Pistachio Milk
        Juice, 199
    Cherry Power, 65
    Red Hurricane, 141
    Sleepy Punch, 242
    Sour Cherry Soda, 305
    Strawberry Cherry
        Soda, 306
    Turmeric Cherry Shot, 278
chia seeds
    Apple, Mint, and Chia
        Juice, 190
    Apple, Orange, and Chia
        Juice, 182
    Blackberry, Pear, and Chia
        Juice, 189
    Blueberry, Grape, and Chia
        Juice, 186
    Carrot, Apricot, and Chia
        Juice, 189
    Carrot, Orange, and Chia
        Juice, 186
    Carrot, Pineapple, and Chia
        Juice, 182
    Cranberry, Apple, Grape,
        and Chia Juice, 180
    Cucumber, Kale, and Chia
        Juice, 181
    Grapefruit, Beet, Apple, and
        Chia Juice, 185
    Grape, Lemon, and Chia
        Juice, 178
    Green Pineapple Chia
        Juice, 192
    introduction to, 17–18
    Mango, Pineapple, and Chia
        Juice, 191
    Mango, Strawberry, and
        Chia Juice, 180
    Orange, Beet, and Chia
        Juice, 192

Peach, Cucumber, and Chia
Juice, 185
Pineapple, Coconut, and
Chia Juice, 181
Raspberry, Apple, and Chia
Juice, 190
Strawberry, Lime, and Chia
Juice, 183
Watermelon, Lime, and
Chia Juice, 178
chile peppers
Chile Lime Shot, 271
Metabolism Booster, 267
Pineapple Hot Stuff, 260
Red Pepper Plush, 40
chlorella, in Super Greens
Shot, 269
cilantro
Carrot Pep-Up, 233
Cilantro Celery Punch, 86
Cilantro Cooler, 80
Cilantro Crush, 75
Green Slammer, 69
Herb Heaven, 93
Herby Green Cleanser, 250
cinnamon
Apple Cinnamon Pecan
Milk Juice, 210
Peach Cinnamon Cashew
Milk Juice, 199
clementines
Clementine Daisy, 132
Lemon Sunburst, 134
cocoa, in Chocolate
Strawberry Cashew Milk
Juice, 203
coconut butter
Simple, Basic Nut Milk, 194
Turmeric Macadamia Milk
Juice, 209
coconut milk
Bahia Cocktail, 150
Hawaiian Sun, 156
introduction to, 18
Pineapple Passion, 153
Pink Goddess, 329
coconut water
ABC Juice, 213
Blueberry, Grape, and Chia
Juice, 186
Brazilian Glow, 150
Caipirinha Crush, 145

Cilantro Cooler, 80
Getaway Cocktail, 149
Ginger Sun, 141
Green Ginger-ade, 340
Golden Breeze, 148
Grapefruit Getaway, 328
Green Goddess, 52
Herby Green Cleanser, 250
introduction to, 18
Mango, Strawberry, and
Chia Juice, 180
Pear Temptation, 152
Pineapple, Coconut, and
Chia Juice, 181
Strawberry, Lime, and Chia
Juice, 183
Wild Watermelon, 221
cranberries
Cranberry, Apple, and Grape
Soda, 302
Cranberry, Apple, and Lime
Punch, 293
Cranberry, Apple, Grape,
and Chia Juice, 180
Cranberry Apple Smash,
102
Cranberry Crush, 96
Cranberry Kiss, 339
Cranberry Vitality, 253
Crazy Cranberry Apple, 223
introduction to, 24
Kale Aces, 54
Orange Cranberry
Punch, 297
cucumbers
Acne Fix, 251
Apple Tango, 339
Bashful Blueberry, 223
Basil Buzz, 73
Beach Babe Bomber, 147
Bedtime Flip, 242
Beet Sunrise, 34
Chard Angel, 61
Cheerful Cherry, 220
Cherry Power, 65
Cilantro Cooler, 80
Clever Cucumber, 225
Cranberry Vitality, 253
Cucumber-ade, 34
Cucumber Apple Fancy, 337
Cucumber Dawn, 59
Cucumber, Grape, and Kale

Punch, 287
Cucumber, Kale, and Chia
Juice, 181
Cucumber Spiral, 332
Dill Angel, 85
Dill Daisy, 89
Dinosaur Power, 219
Electric Cocktail, 236
Garden Glow, 46
Gentle Detox Sipper, 256
Green Apple Twist, 68
Green Craze, 70
Green Fix, 237
Green Ginger-ade, 340
Green Goddess, 52
Green Power Punch, 218
Green Royale, 64
Green Slammer, 69
Green Stimulant, 235
Herb Heaven, 93
Herby Green Cleanser, 250
introduction to, 24–25
Jade Oasis, 59
Jamaica Kiss, 147
Kiwi Smash, 70
Lean Beauty Punch, 263
Mango Tango, 148
Metabolism Booster, 267
Midday Calmer, 244
Minty Green Cocktail, 85
Morning Magic, 236
Parsley Lemonade, 88
Parsley Power, 233
Peaceful Breeze, 245
Peach, Cucumber, and Chia
Juice, 185
Peach, Lemon, and
Cucumber Punch, 296
Pineapple Cucumber
Punch, 296
Radically Red Berry, 219
Raspberry, Apple, and Chia
Juice, 190
Red Reviver, 57
Red Warrior, 47
Skinny Apple Cleanser, 264
Sleepy Punch, 242
Slender Swizzle, 262
Spicy Pear Soda, 314
Star Fruit Spritz, 148
Super Slimmer, 266
Tension Tamer Tonic, 241

Tomato Trim-Down, 264
Veggie Tonic, 45
Wacky Strawberry, 222
Yummy Carrot Craze, 225
Watermelon, Cucumber,
and Mint Punch, 295

dandelion greens, in
Acne Fix, 251
dates
Honeydew Quencher, 327
Simple, Basic Nut Milk, 194
dill
Dill Angel, 85
Dill Daisy, 89
Herby Green Cleanser, 250
Slumber Elixir, 246
dried fruits, 23

Echinacea tincture, in Flu
Buster Shot, 277

fennel
Flaming Fennel, 39
introduction to, 25
flax seeds, 18

garlic
introduction to, 18
Lemon Garlic Shot, 274
Tomato Tonic, 43
ginger
Carrot Apple Warmer, 328
Cilantro Celery Punch, 86
Cold and Flu Shot, 271
Cucumber-ade, 34
Cucumber Dawn, 59
Daytime Detox, 253
Flu Buster Shot, 277
Gingered Peachy Pear
Walnut Milk Juice, 210
Ginger Hot Spot, 60
Ginger Lemonade, 167
Ginger, Lemon, and
Cayenne Shot, 277
Ginger Mixer, 37
Ginger Shot, 271
Ginger Sun, 141
Golden Sun, 126
Grape Oasis, 108
Green Craze, 70
Green Ginger-ade, 340

Hawaiian Sun, 156
Immune Booster Shot, 281
introduction to, 18, 25
Jamaica Kiss, 147
Kale Quencher, 56
Morning Magic, 236
Parsley Power, 233
Raspberry Rambler, 99
Red Beet Ginger Shot, 270
Sage Sunrise, 76
Skinny Sipper, 260
Spicy Apple Ginger
    Soda, 307
Spicy Carrot Tonic, 340
Spicy Citrus Sling, 123
Spicy Orange Mango
    Soda, 308
Spicy Orange Sunrise, 125
Spicy Pear Slim-Down, 267
Spicy Pear Soda, 314
Sweet Flamingo, 333
tips for, 22
Tropic-tini, 146
Waterlime Cooler, 109
Wellness Shot, 280
golden beets, in Citrus
    Fusion, 126
grapefruit
    Bermuda Rose, 150
    Berry Slammer, 130
    Citrus Fusion, 126
    Citrus Zingo, 130
    Daydreamer, 153
    Flaming Orange, 139
    Flat Belly Blast, 266
    Golden Sun, 126
    Grapefruit Apple Soda, 312
    Grapefruit, Beet, Apple, and
        Chia Juice, 185
    Grapefruit Getaway, 328
    Grapefruit Grape
        Punch, 290
    Grapefruit Guzzler, 127
    Grapefruit Lemonade, 169
    Grapefruit Melon
        Punch, 287
    Grapefruit Orange
        Soda, 308
    Grapefruit Sun, 318
    Grapefruit Sunrise, 119
    Green Daisy, 62
    Green Remedy, 65

introduction to, 25
Lime Pucker, 137
Morning Craze, 119
Orange Kiss, 135
Raspberry Aces, 131
Rosemary Grapefruit
    Guzzler, 92
Scarlet Sizzle, 115
Slimming Tonic, 259
Sour Strawberry, 129
Triple Power, 230
grapes
    Apricot Angel, 104
    Awesome Apple, 218
    Blueberry, Grape, and Chia
        Juice, 186
    Blueberry Grape Soda, 304
    Blueberry Sparkle, 114
    Cilantro Celery Punch, 86
    Clever Cucumber, 225
    Cranberry, Apple, and Grape
        Soda, 302
    Cranberry, Apple, Grape,
        and Chia Juice, 180
    Cranberry Apple Smash,
        102
    Cranberry Kiss, 339
    Cucumber, Grape, and Kale
        Punch, 287
    Fruit Flamer, 107
    Gentle Detox Sipper, 256
    Getaway Cocktail, 149
    Grape Apple Soda, 305
    Grapefruit Grape
        Punch, 290
    Grape, Lemon, and Chia
        Juice, 178
    Grape Lucky, 316
    Grape Oasis, 108
    Grape Peach Soda, 301
    Green Grape Celery
        Punch, 292
    introduction to, 25
    Peach Hurricane, 101
    Peachy Cider, 318
    Red Grape Rambler, 322
    Ruby Melone, 147
    Thyme Pineapple Juice, 93
green beans, introduction
    to, 25
green cabbage
    Carrot Kick, 256

Ginger Hot Spot, 60
Sage Booster, 88
green grapes
    Apricot Angel, 104
    Cilantro Celery Punch, 86
    Clever Cucumber, 225
    Cucumber, Grape, and Kale
        Punch, 287
    Grape Apple Soda, 305
    Grapefruit Grape
        Punch, 290
    Grape Peach Soda, 301
    Green Grape Celery
        Punch, 292
    Green Grape Soda, 311
    Jade Oasis, 59
green lettuce
    Daytime Detox, 253
    Green Daisy, 62
    Melon Balancer, 254
greens
    Acne Fix, 251
    carrot greens, 22
    juicing tips, 20
    rhubarb greens, 22

hazelnut milk
    Mango Hazelnut Milk
        Juice, 198
    Strawberry Hazelnut Milk
        Juice, 200
    Sweet Potato Pear Hazelnut
        Milk Juice, 207
honey
    Chocolate Strawberry
        Cashew Milk Juice, 203
    Simple, Basic Nut Milk, 194
honeydew
    Honeydew Quencher, 327
    Honeydew Sour, 110
    Pink Goddess, 329
hot sauce, 17

jalapeño peppers
    Jalapeño Lemonade, 174
    Metabolism Booster, 267
juicers
    centrifugal juicers, 14
    cleaning, 20
    hydraulic press juicers, 15
    manual juicers, 15
    masticating juicers, 20

pulp baskets, 21
single-gear juicers, 14
twin-gear juicers, 14–15
wheatgrass juicers, 15, 230
juicing
    alternating produce, 23
    benefits of, 11–13
    blending compared to, 12
    dried fruits, 23
    empty stomach and, 20
    experimentation, 20
    frozen produce, 23
    greens, 20
    ingredient ratios, 20
    organic produce, 23
    produce preparation, 20
    produce waste, 20–21
    pulp, 21
    storage, 16, 21–22, 339
    tips and tricks, 20–23
    water content, 23

kale
    Apple Slumber, 319
    Citrus Crush, 53
    Cucumber, Grape, and Kale
        Punch, 287
    Cucumber, Kale, and Chia
        Juice, 181
    Daytime Detox, 253
    Dinosaur Power, 219
    Electric Cocktail, 236
    Green Craze, 70
    Green Detoxer, 263
    Green Goddess, 52
    Green Lemonade, 172
    Green Limeade, 66
    Green Royale, 64
    Herby Green Cleanser, 250
    introduction to, 25
    Kale Aces, 54
    Kale Apple Shot, 280
    Kale, Pear, and Turmeric
        Shot, 281
    Kale Quencher, 56
    Morning Magic, 236
    Orange Vitality, 232
    Oregano Royale, 87
    Peaceful Breeze, 245
    Pear Delight, 322
    Pineapple, Coconut, and
        Chia Juice, 181

Red Zing, 233
Ruby Slumber, 46
Triple Power, 230
Veggie-tini, 42
Zucchini Zing, 63
key limes
Citrus Angel, 132
Citrus Zingo, 130
Key Lime Cocktail, 120
Lime Pucker, 137
kiwifruit
Bedtime Flip, 242
Blackberry Bliss, 113
Kiwi Divine, 156
Kiwi Lemonade, 172
Kiwi Mint-ade, 79
Kiwi Pear Soda, 311
Kiwi Smash, 70
Kiwi-tini, 323
Mandarin Plush, 135
Rosemary Watermelon
  Crush, 90
Super Celery Cooler, 215
Tropical Craze, 319

lemons
Acne Fix, 251
Apple Flip, 112
Apple, Mint, and Chia
  Juice, 190
Apple Slumber, 319
Basil Buzz, 73
Basil Strawberry
  Lemonade, 161
Beach Babe Bomber, 147
Beet Sunrise, 34
Blackberry Mint
  Lemonade, 168
Blueberry Lemonade, 158
Carrot Crush, 31
Carrot Dandy, 42
Carrot Lemonade, 175
Carrot, Lemon, and
  Pineapple Punch, 289
Celery Reviver, 249
Cherry Lemonade, 171
Cilantro Celery Punch, 86
Cilantro Cooler, 80
Citrus Angel, 132
Citrus Buzz, 125
Cranberry Vitality, 253
Cucumber-ade, 34
Cucumber Dawn, 59

Daydreamer, 153
Daytime Detox, 253
Dill Daisy, 89
Flaming Orange, 139
Flu Buster Shot, 277
Gentle Detox Sipper, 256
Getaway Cocktail, 149
Ginger Lemonade, 167
Ginger, Lemon, and
  Cayenne Shot, 277
Golden Breeze, 148
Grapefruit Lemonade, 169
Grape, Lemon, and Chia
  Juice, 178
Grape Lucky, 316
Grape Oasis, 108
Green Ginger-ade, 340
Green Lemonade, 172
Green Limeade, 66
Immune Booster Shot, 281
introduction to, 18, 25–26
Jalapeño Lemonade, 174
Key Lime Cocktail, 120
Kiwi Lemonade, 172
Lemon Alkalizer, 259
Lemon, Apple, and Beet
  Punch, 284
Lemon-berry Sunburst, 340
Lemon Buzz, 321
Lemon Garlic Shot, 274
Lemon Lime Ale, 123
Lemon, Lime, and Pineapple
  Punch, 291
Lemon, Lime, Pineapple,
  and Raspberry Punch, 295
Lemon Meringue, 138
Lemon Sunburst, 134
Lime Mint Lemonade, 175
Lime Zing, 239
Lovely Lemon, 220
Melon Rosa, 332
Metabolism Booster, 267
Orange Lemonade, 160
Orange Swinger, 331
Parsley Lemonade, 88
Parsley Power, 233
Peaceful Breeze, 245
Peach Hurricane, 101
Peach Lemonade, 169
Peach, Lemon, and
  Cucumber Punch, 296
Pear Lemonade, 158
Pineapple Lemonade, 174

Pineapple Sunshine, 120
Pink Sunburst, 126
Pink Zing, 100
Purple Daisy, 48
Raspberry Lemonade, 161
Raspberry Lemon Soda, 307
Raspberry Mint
  Lemonade, 163
Red Beet Lemonade, 171
Red Beet Lemon Shot, 273
Red Melon-tini, 154
Rosemary Lemonade, 166
Rose Royale, 129
Skinny Mini Cocktail, 258
Skinny Sipper, 260
Strawberry Lemonade, 163
Super Slimmer, 266
Sweet Lemonade, 159
Sweet Lime Lemonade, 164
Sweet Thyme Rosemary
  Punch, 89
Tangerine Peach
  Lemonade, 164
Tarragon Lemon-ale, 86
Tart Apple Soda, 305
Turmeric Lemon Shot, 274
Watermelon Lemonade,
  168
Watermelon, Raspberry, and
  Lemon Punch, 292
Watermelon Strawberry
  Lemonade, 166
Wellness Shot, 280
lettuce
Broccoli Balancer, 53
Broccoli Breeze, 63
Caribbean Night, 142
Chard Angel, 61
Citrus Angel, 132
Cucumber Dawn, 59
Daytime Detox, 253
Ginger Hot Spot, 60
Green Apple Twist, 68
Green Cider, 54
Green Daisy, 62
Green Fix, 237
Green Goddess, 52
Green Julep, 81
Green Melon Glow, 322
Green Pineapple Chia
  Juice, 192
Lemon Alkalizer, 259
Melon Balancer, 254

Mint-ade, 51
Morning Magic, 236
Parsley Plush, 82
Pineapple Kick, 230
limes
Caipirinha Crush, 145
Cherry Craze, 104
Chile Lime Shot, 271
Citrus Angel, 132
Citrus Breakfast, 127
Citrus Buzz, 125
Citrus Zingo, 130
Constipation Reliever, 251
Cranberry, Apple, and Lime
  Punch, 293
Cucumber-ade, 34
Cucumber Apple Fancy, 337
Dinosaur Power, 219
Flat Belly Blast, 266
Fruit Flamer, 107
Ginger Sun, 141
Golden Sun, 126
Grapefruit Sun, 318
Green Craze, 70
Green Fix, 237
Green Glory, 48
Green Julep, 81
Green Limeade, 66
Green Pineapple Chia
  Juice, 192
Green Sipper, 324
Green Slammer, 69
Honeydew Quencher, 327
Honeydew Sour, 110
introduction to, 18
Kale Quencher, 56
Key Lime Cocktail, 120
Lemon Lime Ale, 123
Lemon, Lime, and Pineapple
  Punch, 291
Lemon, Lime, Pineapple,
  and Raspberry Punch, 295
Lime Mint Lemonade, 175
Lime Pucker, 137
Lime Zing, 239
Mandarin Plush, 135
Mango Fusion, 69
Mango Tango, 148
Melon Zingo, 108
Mighty Mango, 226
Mint-ade, 51
Minty Green Cocktail, 85
Peach-tastic, 102

Pear Temptation, 152
Pineapple Bombshell, 142
Pineapple Hot Stuff, 260
Pineapple Passion, 153
Raspberry Pear Punch, 327
Relax-tini, 244
Ruby Melone, 147
Sage Booster, 88
Slender Swizzle, 262
Sour Apple Soda, 301
Sour Cherry Soda, 305
Spearmint Sour, 90
Strawberry Basil Blush, 73
Strawberry, Lime, and Chia
    Juice, 183
Strawberry, Lime, and Pear
    Punch, 284
Sweet Lime Lemonade, 164
Veggie Tonic, 45
Waterlime Cooler, 109
Watermelon, Lime, and
    Chia Juice, 178
Watermelon Sling, 318

macadamia milk
    Blueberry Macadamia Milk
        Juice, 204
    Turmeric Macadamia Milk
        Juice, 209
maca powder, 18
mangoes
    Carrot Mango Cashew Milk
        Juice, 209
    Exotic Oasis, 145
    Fruity Parsley Punch, 79
    Jamaica Kiss, 147
    Mango Fix, 321
    Mango Fusion, 69
    Mango Hazelnut Milk
        Juice, 198
    Mango, Pineapple, and Chia
        Juice, 191
    Mango, Strawberry, and
        Chia Juice, 180
    Mango Tango, 148
    Mango Viva, 154
    Mighty Mango, 226
    Orange Kiss, 135
    Orange Mango Punch, 285
    peeling, 22
    Pineapple, Mango, and
        Carrot Punch, 288
    Pineapple Passion, 153

Red Hurricane, 141
Spicy Citrus Sling, 123
Spicy Orange Mango
    Soda, 308
Strawberry Mango Cashew
    Milk Juice, 200
Strawberry Twist, 324
Tomato Dream, 336
Tropical Craze, 319
Tropic-tini, 146
maple syrup, in Simple,
    Basic Nut Milk, 194
mint
    Apple, Mint, and Chia
        Juice, 190
    Blackberry Mint
        Lemonade, 168
    Exotic Oasis, 145
    Grapefruit Sun, 318
    Green Ginger-ade, 340
    Green Julep, 81
    Kiwi Mint-ade, 79
    Lime Mint Lemonade, 175
    Mint-ade, 51
    Mint Melody, 75
    Minty Green Cocktail, 85
    Pear Delight, 322
    Raspberry Mint
        Lemonade, 163
    Red Melon-tini, 154
    Watermelon, Cucumber,
        and Mint Punch, 295

nectarines, in Green Royale,
    64

orange bell pepper, in
    Cayenne Kicker, 34
oranges
    All-Star Favorite, 216
    Apple, Orange, and Chia
        Juice, 182
    Bahia Cocktail, 150
    Blood Orange Cocktail, 122
    Caribbean Night, 142
    Carrot, Orange, and Chia
        Juice, 186
    Carrot Orange Swirl, 331
    Chard Booster, 60
    Citrus Angel, 132
    Citrus Breakfast, 127
    Citrus Buzz, 125
    Citrus Crush, 53

Citrus Fusion, 126
Citrus Royale, 99
Citrus Zingo, 130
Clementine Daisy, 132
Cold and Flu Shot, 271
Daydreamer, 153
Flaming Orange, 139
Fruity Parsley Punch, 79
Golden Sun, 126
Grapefruit Getaway, 328
Grapefruit Orange
    Soda, 308
Green Royale, 64
introduction to, 26
Joyful Jamberry, 220
Lemon Meringue, 138
Mandarin Plush, 135
Melon Rosa, 332
Melon Twist, 138
Mighty Mango, 226
Morning Craze, 119
Orange, Beet, and Chia
    Juice, 192
Orangeberry Oasis, 137
Orange Cranberry
    Punch, 297
Orange Kiss, 135
Orange Lemonade, 160
Orange Mango Punch, 285
Orange Pineapple
    Punch, 291
Orange Slumber, 117
Orange Snap, 128
Orange Swinger, 331
Orange Vitality, 232
Orange Zing, 33
Persimmon Twist, 107
Pineapple Nectar, 316
Pineapple Passion, 153
Pink Sunburst, 126
Purple Cocktail, 113
Raspberry Aces, 131
Red Beet, Orange, and
    Apple Punch, 288
Red Grape Rambler, 322
Red Hurricane, 141
Rose Punch, 97
Rose Royale, 129
Spicy Citrus Sling, 123
Spicy Orange Mango
    Soda, 308
Spicy Orange Sunrise, 125
Spinach Power, 249

Strawberry Orange Soda,
    304
Stress-Free Cocktail, 241
Sweet Flamingo, 333
Sweet Orange Soda, 300
Sweet Thyme Rosemary
    Punch, 89
Tangerine Tang, 227
Tomato Dream, 336
Tropic-tini, 146
oregano
    Immune Booster Shot, 281
    Oregano Oasis, 76
    Oregano Royale, 87
organic produce, 23

papaya
    Carrot Papaya Punch, 326
    Papaya Dawn, 117
    peeling, 22
    Red Hurricane, 141
    Sweet Flamingo, 333
parsley
    Emerald Energizer, 57
    Energy Cocktail, 33
    Fruity Parsley Punch, 79
    Green Jolt, 230
    Herb Heaven, 93
    Herby Green Cleanser, 250
    introduction to, 26
    Mango Fix, 321
    Parsley Lemonade, 88
    Parsley Plush, 82
    Parsley Power, 233
    Sweet Potato Buzz, 235
    Veg Crush, 39
    Veggie Starlet, 32
    Veggie-tini, 42
parsnips
    Broccoli Breeze, 63
    Parsnip Parfait, 45
    Scarlet Night, 46
peaches
    Cucumber Spiral, 332
    Fruit Flamer, 107
    Gingered Peachy Pear
        Walnut Milk Juice, 210
    Grape Peach Soda, 301
    Green Heaven, 321
    Peach Cinnamon Cashew
        Milk Juice, 199
    Peach, Cucumber, and Chia
        Juice, 185

Peach Hurricane, 101
Peach Lemonade, 169
Peach, Lemon, and
    Cucumber Punch, 296
Peach Pecan Milk Juice, 197
Peach Pistachio Milk
    Juice, 203
Peach-tastic, 102
Peachy Cider, 318
Pineapple Peach Party, 334
Tangerine Peach Lemonade,
    164
pears
    Apricot Angel, 104
    Berry Fix, 114
    Blackberry Bliss, 113
    Blackberry, Pear, and Chia
        Juice, 189
    Broccoli Balancer, 53
    Caribbean Night, 142
    Carrot Rosemary
        Cocktail, 80
    Cheerful Cherry, 220
    Constipation Reliever, 251
    Cranberry Crush, 96
    Electric Cocktail, 236
    Fantastic Pear Punch, 226
    Flaming Fennel, 39
    Gingered Peachy Pear
        Walnut Milk Juice, 210
    Ginger Hot Spot, 60
    Green Daisy, 62
    Green Fix, 237
    Green Heaven, 321
    Green Power Punch, 218
    Green Swizzle, 51
    Herb Heaven, 93
    introduction to, 26
    Kale, Pear, and Turmeric
        Shot, 281
    Kiwi Pear Soda, 311
    Lemon-berry Sunburst, 340
    Lime Pucker, 137
    Minty Green Cocktail, 85
    Morning Magic, 236
    Parsley Lemonade, 88
    Parsley Plush, 82
    Peach Lemonade, 169
    Pear Apple Soda, 301
    Pear Delight, 322
    Pear Lemonade, 158
    Pear Plush, 96
    Pear Temptation, 152

Pear Walnut Milk Juice, 208
Popeye Punch, 215
Purple Daisy, 48
Raspberry Pear Punch, 327
Rosemary Slammer, 83
Sage Booster, 88
Sage Sunrise, 76
seeds, 21
Skinny Apple Cleanser, 264
Slumber Elixir, 246
Spicy Pear Slim-Down, 267
Spicy Pear Soda, 314
Strawberry Cherry
    Soda, 306
Strawberry, Lime, and Pear
    Punch, 284
Sweet Potato Pear Hazelnut
    Milk Juice, 207
Tarragon Lemon-ale, 86
Tension Tamer Tonic, 241
Yummy Carrot Craze, 225
pecan milk
    Apple Cinnamon Pecan
        Milk Juice, 210
    Peach Pecan Milk Juice, 197
    Pineapple Apricot Pecan
        Milk Juice, 208
peels, 21, 22, 171, 253
pepper, 19
persimmons
    Caribbean Night, 142
    Persimmon Twist, 107
pineapple
    Bahia Cocktail, 150
    Blackberry Pineapple
        Punch, 293
    Cantaloupe Blush, 101
    Caribbean Night, 142
    Carrot Kick, 256
    Carrot, Lemon, and
        Pineapple Punch, 289
    Carrot Orange Swirl, 331
    Carrot, Pineapple, and Chia
        Juice, 182
    Cherry Craze, 104
    Citrus Royale, 99
    Exotic Oasis, 145
    Grapefruit Guzzler, 127
    Green Monster, 222
    Green Pineapple Chia
        Juice, 192
    Hawaiian Sun, 156
    introduction to, 26

Kale Aces, 54
Kiwi Mint-ade, 79
Lemon Buzz, 321
Lemon, Lime, and Pineapple
    Punch, 291
Lemon, Lime, Pineapple,
    and Raspberry Punch, 295
Magical Melon, 218
Mango, Pineapple, and Chia
    Juice, 191
Mango Tango, 148
Melon Zingo, 108
Mint Melody, 75
Orangeberry Oasis, 137
Orange Pineapple
    Punch, 291
Orange Slumber, 117
Orange Snap, 128
Parsley Plush, 82
Pineapple Apricot Pecan
    Milk Juice, 208
Pineapple Bombshell, 142
Pineapple Cashew Milk
    Juice, 198
Pineapple, Coconut, and
    Chia Juice, 181
Pineapple Cucumber
    Punch, 296
Pineapple Dawn, 40
Pineapple Flip, 56
Pineapple Hot Stuff, 260
Pineapple Kick, 230
Pineapple Lemonade, 174
Pineapple Lime Soda, 299
Pineapple, Mango, and
    Carrot Punch, 288
Pineapple Nectar, 316
Pineapple Passion, 153
Pineapple Peach Party, 334
Pineapple Raspberry
    Soda, 312
Pineapple Soda, 302
Pineapple Spearmint
    Cooler, 92
Pineapple Sunshine, 120
Pineapple Wheatgrass
    Shot, 269
Popeye Punch, 215
Purple Cocktail, 113
Spicy Carrot Tonic, 340
Sunny Swizzle, 154
Sweet Sunrise, 66
Tarragon Cocktail, 83

Thyme Pineapple Juice, 93
Tranquil Toddy, 245
Tropical Craze, 319
Veggie-tini, 42
Yellow Sling, 97
Zucchini Zing, 63
pistachio milk
    Cherry Pistachio Milk
        Juice, 199
    Mixed-Berry Pistachio Milk
        Juice, 197
    Peach Pistachio Milk
        Juice, 203
pomegranate
    Apple Pomegranate
        Soda, 299
    Pomegranate Cider, 105
    Rose Royale, 129
potatoes
    Cilantro Crush, 75
    Energy Cocktail, 33
psyllium husk, 19
purple cabbage
    Purple Cocktail, 113
    Purple Daisy, 48
purple grapes, in Grape
    Oasis, 108

radishes
    Radical Radish, 216
    Veg Royale, 31
raspberries
    Bermuda Rose, 150
    Berry Fix, 114
    Lemon-berry Sunburst, 340
    Lemon, Lime, Pineapple,
        and Raspberry Punch, 295
    Mixed-Berry Pistachio Milk
        Juice, 197
    Pineapple Raspberry
        Soda, 312
    Pink Goddess, 329
    Pink Parfait, 110
    Radically Red Berry, 219
    Raspberry Aces, 131
    Raspberry Almond Milk
        Juice, 198
    Raspberry, Apple, and Chia
        Juice, 190
    Raspberry Lemonade, 161
    Raspberry Lemon Soda, 307
    Raspberry Mint Lemonade,
        163

Raspberry Pear Punch, 327
Raspberry Rambler, 99
Red Rainbow Juice, 213
Sleepy Punch, 242
Watermelon, Raspberry, and
    Lemon Punch, 292
Wild Watermelon, 221
red apples
    Crazy Cranberry Apple, 223
    Strawberry Basil Blush, 73
red beets
    Lemon, Apple, and Beet
        Punch, 284
    Red Beet Ginger Shot, 270
    Red Beet Lemonade, 171
    Red Beet, Orange, and
        Apple Punch, 288
    Red Reviver, 57
    Red Zing, 233
    Ruby Slumber, 46
red bell pepper
    Carrot Pep-Up, 233
    Cayenne Kicker, 34
    Clementine Daisy, 132
    Oregano Royale, 87
    Red Cadillac, 48
    Red Pepper Plush, 40
    Veg Crush, 39
red cabbage
    Detox Shot, 275
    Red Cabbage Apple
        Shot, 278
red grapefruit, in Bermuda
    Rose, 150
red grapes
    Blueberry Grape Soda, 304
    Blueberry Sparkle, 114
    Cranberry, Apple, and Grape
        Soda, 302
    Grape, Lemon, and Chia
        Juice, 178
    Grape Oasis, 108
    Peach Hurricane, 101
    Red Grape Rambler, 322
rhubarb greens, avoiding, 22
romaine lettuce
    Broccoli Balancer, 53
    Broccoli Breeze, 63
    Caribbean Night, 142
    Chard Angel, 61
    Citrus Angel, 132
    Cucumber Dawn, 59
    Daytime Detox, 253

Ginger Hot Spot, 60
Green Apple Twist, 68
Green Cider, 54
Green Fix, 237
Green Goddess, 52
Green Julep, 81
Green Melon Glow, 322
Green Pineapple Chia
    Juice, 192
introduction to, 26
Lemon Alkalizer, 259
Mint-ade, 51
Morning Magic, 236
Parsley Plush, 82
Pineapple Kick, 230
rosemary
    Carrot Rosemary
        Cocktail, 80
    Rosemary Grapefruit
        Guzzler, 92
    Rosemary Lemonade, 166
    Rosemary Slammer, 83
    Rosemary Watermelon
        Crush, 90
    Sweet Thyme Rosemary
        Punch, 89

sage
    Herb Heaven, 93
    Sage Booster, 88
    Sage Sunrise, 76
    Tension Tamer Tonic, 241
Simple, Basic Nut Milk
    Apple Cinnamon Pecan
        Milk Juice, 210
    Apricot Almond Milk
        Juice, 202
    Bahia Cocktail, 150
    Blackberry Vanilla Cashew
        Milk Juice, 204
    Blueberry Almond Milk
        Juice, 195
    Blueberry Macadamia Milk
        Juice, 204
    Carrot Almond Milk
        Juice, 195
    Carrot Cashew Milk
        Juice, 207
    Carrot Mango Cashew Milk
        Juice, 209
    Cherry Pistachio Milk
        Juice, 199
    Chocolate Strawberry

Cashew Milk Juice, 203
Gingered Peachy Pear
    Walnut Milk Juice, 210
Hawaiian Sun, 156
Mango Hazelnut Milk
    Juice, 198
Mixed-Berry Pistachio Milk
    Juice, 197
Peach Cinnamon Cashew
    Milk Juice, 199
Peach Pecan Milk Juice, 197
Peach Pistachio Milk
    Juice, 203
Pear Walnut Milk Juice, 208
Pineapple Apricot Pecan
    Milk Juice, 208
Pineapple Cashew Milk
    Juice, 198
Pineapple Passion, 153
Pink Goddess, 329
Raspberry Almond Milk
    Juice, 198
recipe, 194
Strawberry Almond Milk
    Juice, 201
Strawberry Hazelnut Milk
    Juice, 200
Strawberry Mango Cashew
    Milk Juice, 200
Sweet Potato Pear Hazelnut
    Milk Juice, 207
Turmeric Macadamia Milk
    Juice, 209
sparkling water
    Apple Pomegranate
        Soda, 299
    Blackberry Apple Soda, 314
    Blueberry Grape Soda, 304
    Cranberry, Apple, and Grape
        Soda, 302
    Grape Apple Soda, 305
    Grapefruit Apple Soda, 312
    Grapefruit Orange
        Soda, 308
    Grape Peach Soda, 301
    Green Grape Soda, 311
    introduction to, 19
    Kiwi Pear Soda, 311
    Pear Apple Soda, 301
    Pineapple Raspberry
        Soda, 312
    Pineapple Soda, 302
    Raspberry Lemon Soda, 307

Sour Apple Soda, 301
Sour Cherry Soda, 305
Spicy Apple Ginger
    Soda, 307
Spicy Orange Mango
    Soda, 298
Spicy Pear Soda, 314
Strawberry Cherry
    Soda, 306
Strawberry Orange
    Soda, 304
Sweet Orange Soda, 300
Tart Apple Soda, 305
Watermelon Soda, 313
spearmint
    Pineapple Spearmint
        Cooler, 92
    Spearmint Sour, 90
spinach
    Constipation Reliever, 251
    Dill Daisy, 89
    Dinosaur Power, 219
    Energy Elixir, 239
    Golden Sunset, 47
    Green Fix, 237
    Green Ginger-ade, 340
    Green Heaven, 321
    Green Remedy, 65
    Green Sipper, 324
    Green Slammer, 69
    Green Swizzle, 51
    introduction to, 26
    Kiwi Smash, 70
    Minty Green Cocktail, 85
    Pineapple Peach Party, 334
    Popeye Punch, 215
    Red Reviver, 57
    Slumber Elixir, 246
    Spinach Power, 249
    Sweet Sunrise, 66
    Tranquil Toddy, 245
    Veg Royale, 31
spirulina
    introduction to, 19
    Lime Zing, 239
    Spirulina Apple Shot, 273
    Super Greens Shot, 269
storage, 16, 21–22, 339
strawberries
    Basil Strawberry
        Lemonade, 161
    Beach Babe Bomber, 147
    Berry Fix, 114

Bodacious Berry, 222
Brazilian Glow, 150
Chard Angel, 61
Chard Booster, 60
Chocolate Strawberry
  Cashew Milk Juice, 203
Citrus Zingo, 130
Cucumber Spiral, 332
Daydreamer, 153
Electric Cocktail, 236
Flat Belly Blast, 266
Fruit Flamer, 107
Ginger Sun, 141
introduction to, 26–27
Joyful Jamberry, 220
Kiwi Divine, 156
Lemon Sunburst, 134
Magical Melon, 218
Mango, Strawberry, and
  Chia Juice, 180
Morning Craze, 119
Papaya Dawn, 117
Pink Goddess, 329
Pink Melon-ade, 96
Radically Red Berry, 219
Rosemary Watermelon
  Crush, 90
Rose Punch, 97
Sour Strawberry, 129
Spinach Power, 249
Star Fruit Spritz, 148
Strawberry Almond Milk
  Juice, 201
Strawberry Basil Blush, 73
Strawberry Cherry
  Soda, 306
Strawberry Hazelnut Milk
  Juice, 200
Strawberry Lemonade, 163
Strawberry, Lime, and Chia
  Juice, 183
Strawberry, Lime, and Pear
  Punch, 284
Strawberry Mango Cashew
  Milk Juice, 200
Strawberry Orange
  Soda, 304
Strawberry Twist, 324
Stress-Free Cocktail, 241
Wacky Strawberry, 222
Watermelon Strawberry
  Lemonade, 166

sweet potatoes
  Chard Booster, 60
  Citrus Royale, 99
  Electric Cocktail, 236
  introduction to, 27
  Red Cadillac, 48
  Sweet Potato Buzz, 235
  Sweet Potato Pear Hazelnut
    Milk Juice, 207
  Sweet Potato Sunshine, 37
  Sweet Sunrise, 66
Swiss chard
  Chard Angel, 61
  Chard Booster, 60
  introduction to, 27
  Midday Calmer, 244

tangerines
  Ginger Sun, 141
  Pink Sunburst, 126
  Tangerine Peach
    Lemonade, 164
  Tangerine Tang, 227
tarragon
  Peaceful Breeze, 245
  Tarragon Cocktail, 83
  Tarragon Lemon-ale, 86
thyme
  Sweet Thyme Rosemary
    Punch, 89
  Thyme Pineapple Juice, 93
  Thyme Toddy, 78
tomatoes
  Cayenne Kicker, 34
  Celery Reviver, 249
  Dill Daisy, 89
  introduction to, 27
  Orange Zing, 33
  Red Cardinal, 337
  Red Pepper Plush, 40
  Scarlet Night, 46
  Tomato Dream, 336
  Tomato Tonic, 43
  Tomato Trim-Down, 264
  V6 Juice, 40
  Veggie Tonic, 45
  Veg Royale, 31
tools
  cutting boards, 16
  glass jars, 16
  glass straws, 16
  Mason jars, 16

measuring cups, 16
peelers, 16
salad spinners, 16
sharp knives, 16
strainers, 17
vegetable brushes, 17
turmeric
  Carrot, Orange, and Chia
    Juice, 186
  Green Craze, 70
  introduction to, 19, 27
  Kale, Pear, and Turmeric
    Shot, 281
  Spicy Carrot Tonic, 340
  Spicy Citrus Sling, 123
  Turmeric Cherry Shot, 278
  Turmeric Lemon Shot, 274
  Turmeric Macadamia Milk
    Juice, 209

vanilla
  Blackberry Vanilla Cashew
    Milk Juice, 204
  Simple, Basic Nut Milk, 194
vinegar soaks, 17

walnut milk
  Gingered Peachy Pear
    Walnut Milk Juice, 210
  Pear Walnut Milk Juice, 208
watercress
  Cherry Power, 65
  Green Stimulant, 235
  Peaceful Breeze, 245
  Pineapple Flip, 56
watermelon
  Cheerful Cherry, 220
  Cranberry Kiss, 339
  Grapefruit Melon
    Punch, 287
  Green Melon Glow, 322
  introduction to, 27
  Melon Balancer, 254
  Melon Hurricane, 334
  Melon Rosa, 332
  Melon Zingo, 108
  Pink Zing, 100
  Red Melon-tini, 154
  Red Rainbow Juice, 213
  Rosemary Watermelon
    Crush, 90
  Skinny Mini Cocktail, 258

Sunny Swizzle, 154
Waterlime Cooler, 109
Watermelon, Cucumber,
  and Mint Punch, 295
Watermelon Lemonade,
  168
Watermelon, Lime, and
  Chia Juice, 178
Watermelon, Raspberry, and
  Lemon Punch, 292
Watermelon Sling, 318
Watermelon Soda, 313
Watermelon Strawberry
  Lemonade, 166
Wild Watermelon, 221
wheatgrass
  introduction to, 20, 27
  juicers for, 15, 230
  Pineapple Kick, 230
  Pineapple Wheatgrass
    Shot, 269
  Red Warrior, 47
  Super Greens Shot, 269
  Wheatgrass Reviver, 232

yellow bell pepper
  Oregano Royale, 87
  Skinny Sipper, 260
  Tomato Trim-Down, 264
  Yellow Sling, 97

zucchini
  Beet-ade, 62
  Carrot Dandy, 42
  Chard Angel, 61
  Green Detoxer, 263
  Green Slammer, 69
  introduction to, 27
  Mango Fusion, 69
  Zucchini Zing, 63